SHE LED THE WAY

STORIES OF BLACK WOMEN WHO CHANGED HISTORY

SUZANNE CURTIS BRIGGS

Revell

a division of Baker Publishing Group
Grand Rapids, Michigan

Published by Revell
a division of Baker Publishing Group
PO Box 6287, Grand Rapids, MI 49516-6287
www.revellbooks.com

Printed in the United States of America

Library of Congress Cataloging-in-Publication Data
Names: Briggs, Suzanne Curtis, 1953– author.
Title: She led the way : stories of Black women who changed history / Suzanne Curtis Briggs.
Description: Grand Rapids, MI : Revell, a division of Baker Publishing Group, [2022]
Identifiers: LCCN 2021047542 | ISBN 9780800741983 (casebound) | ISBN 9780800735913 (paperback) | ISBN 9781493436194 (ebook)
Subjects: LCSH: African American women—Biography. | African American women—Religious life. | Christian life—United States—History. | United States—Race relations—History.
Classification: LCC E185.96 .B8295 2022 | DDC 920.72/08996073—dc23/eng/20211018
LC record available at https://lccn.loc.gov/2021047542

Illustrations by Octavia Ink of Pretty In Ink.

Baker Publishing Group publications use paper produced from sustainable forestry practices and post-consumer waste whenever possible.

22 23 24 25 26 27 28   7 6 5 4 3 2 1

CONTENTS

Contents

A WORD TO THE READER

I've loved to read ever since I learned how. Maybe that's true for you too! I grew up reading fiction (especially mysteries), books about historical events, books on social issues, poetry, the Bible, travel stories, animal stories—really just about everything. My very favorite things to read, however, were biographies of American heroes and heroines, and that's still true for me today.

So what a pleasure it is for me to introduce you to fourteen Black American women who lived in times ranging from before the Civil War on into the twenty-first century—women who started life in ordinary ways and grew up to be extraordinary. Women who found why they were here. Women of faith and courage. Women who achieved mighty things and then led the way for others.

Today, I see an increasing hunger in our culture to know and see Black women. We read many more bestselling books by or about Black women. Dramatic productions with Black actresses and Black female directors are on stage and television and movie screens everywhere. More Black women hold office. More Black women are in the world of sports. We are more likely to see a Black woman reporting or commenting on the news of the day than ever before. So it's been so exciting for me to get absorbed in the lives of these fourteen remarkable Black women.

You'll read about their beginnings, their struggles, their victories, and their legacies. In my opinion, that's the best way to learn our history—to read and understand the stories of very real, flesh-and-blood people who starred in the events of their times.

These women worked hard for what they accomplished. They overcame obstacles, some due to race and some due to gender. They achieved much. And yet none of these women appeared out of nowhere. They all followed in the footsteps of Black women who went before them. They benefited from those legacies.

What they gained they in turn passed on to the next generation in so many ways.

Our subjects will be presented in the order of their birth year. Each woman's profile starts with a brief story from when she was a girl. Then we'll go through her life. We'll learn about her influences. We'll learn about her gifts. We'll learn how she led the way for others. Following each profile are a few questions and suggestions for you to enhance your understanding, either alone or with a group.

As you read, perhaps you'll want to learn more about one of these women. The library is full of books and stories about them. There are movies too, and sometimes more than one movie per person. Remember, however, that Hollywood seldom tells a completely accurate story. They sell drama, after all, so they often make some of it up or leave something out.

Online you can also find more. There are true slave narratives on the internet—autobiographies a few of these women and so many others wrote themselves, giving us a clear, firsthand account of life during the years of slavery. There are video and audio clips of some of the women being interviewed. You can find many more fascinating details about these women than we can fit in one book.

To help you go further, at the end of the book are lists of the sources I used for each subject, which can give you more insight into a woman and her character. You may find the facts from different sources don't always agree, and this is especially true for anyone with a celebrity status. When that happened in my research, I chose to include what I considered the most plausible version of events.

There is one more thing to remember as you delve into the lives of our subjects: nobody's perfect. These women were human beings, just like all of us. They were heroines, not deities. They made mistakes, just like we do.

I hope you enjoy meeting these women as much as I enjoyed writing about them. They are amazing human beings who found their purpose. They held strong. They persevered. They followed the path they believed God laid out for them.

And then they led the way for others.

Suzanne Curtis Briggs

ELLEN CRAFT

(1826–1891)

Escapee from Slavery and Memoirist

"Since my escape from slavery, I have gotten much better in every respect than I could have possibly anticipated."

The wagon rocked along the rutted road, pulled by an unperturbed mule. The elderly Black driver held the reins loosely in his hands, and next to him sat an eleven-year-old girl whose slight body bounced on the wooden seat. She wore a faded cotton skirt and blouse, both a little too large for her, and a colorful scarf she had wound around her head like her mother did.

The child clutched the seat. She'd been taken from her mother early in the morning to be driven away from the only home she'd ever known. She was going to a different plantation to live, and she didn't know when she might see her mother again. The new plantation was only a couple of hours away by mule, but since this child was a slave, she would have no way or even any right to visit her mother in the future.

The girl in the wagon had another unique burden. She was a slave who looked white. She was born with very light skin, pale eyes, and naturally straight hair. In fact, she looked as white as any Caucasian person, and for a slave that was not a good thing.

Today the girl in the wagon was taking with her some special skills. Momma had taught her young, shy daughter how to sew—and very well, even at age eleven. In the 1800s, all clothing was handmade, and a good seamstress was worth a great deal to ladies on plantations. As was the case for her mother, the daughter's sewing abilities meant she could perform her specialty work indoors instead of laboring outdoors in all kinds of Georgia weather. But while this meant an easier working life for her, she was still enslaved. She still had no control over her own life.

Another skill the girl in the wagon was taking with her to the new plantation was how to get along among people. It was imperative for slaves to know what was going on around them, and she became especially observant, quietly watching, listening to what was said, and, in some cases, figuring out what was not said. Since she looked so different from the other slaves, she had learned how to not draw unwanted attention to herself. She covered her straight hair with a scarf and moved about quickly and quietly.

Little did the girl in the wagon know that her appearance was going to be her ticket out of a life of enslavement. She could not know that she would marry a good man, and that together they would dream up a daring and dramatic plan of escape—a plan requiring the quiet young wife to become an actress for a few days. She would need to pretend to be someone she was not, in both her looks and her actions. She would also put her exceptional needlework skills to use.

Of course, the girl in the wagon knew none of this as she jostled on the wooden seat. She simply hoped she'd get a chance to see her mother again. That was as much of the future as she could think about for the time being.

———

Ellen Craft was born in Macon, Georgia, in 1826, a time when the state of Georgia was well on its way to having the most slaves and slaveholders of any state in the Deep South. Ellen's father was the master of the plantation, but she did not live in her father's home. Since

> **"I had much rather starve in England, a free woman, than be a slave for the best man that ever breathed upon the American continent."**

her mother was a slave, Ellen was a slave, and they lived in one of the cabins clustered away from the main house.

Ellen's slaveholding father was white, and her enslaved mother was half Black, half white. Ellen was born with straight hair and with skin and eyes so pale she looked like a white person. In fact, she resembled her father so much that the man's wife, the mistress of the plantation, was furious every time she looked at Ellen. The mistress did not want people to think this white-appearing slave child was one of her own, and she was determined to get her out of sight.

This situation was not only awkward for Ellen but also potentially dangerous for her. At any time, the master or his wife could sell her or her mother away to another plantation. Of course, this threat of being sold was true for all enslaved people. But since Ellen looked so much like her father, it was clearly only a matter of time before something unfortunate might happen to her.

But the mistress did not sell her. Instead, once she'd had enough of seeing Ellen around, she gave her to her eighteen-year-old daughter as a wedding present. The daughter, named Eliza, had recently married and moved away. The fact that a human being could be a wedding gift was only too normal in those days. But at least once Ellen moved to Eliza's home, she would be safe from being sold—for now.

Eliza was young and fairly kind to Ellen. Of course, the new young mistress was actually Ellen's half sister. They looked alike, and even their names were similar—Ellen and Eliza. But nobody spoke about it. From the beginning, Ellen was a personal maid to Eliza, helping her bathe and dress. Ellen also did light housework in the upstairs of the large plantation house, ran errands, and was Eliza's seamstress.

By the time Ellen was through her teens, she was such an accomplished seamstress that Eliza gave her a small cottage to use. Ellen was left alone to live and work quietly in this cottage that contained all the fabrics and sewing tools she used. This kind of arrangement was rare. Maybe Eliza knew Ellen was her half sister or maybe she just liked the dresses Ellen could produce. At any rate, the arrangement suited Ellen well.

Something momentous happened when Ellen was twenty years old. She fell in love with a young cabinetmaker on the plantation named William Craft. A picture Ellen carried in her locket showed that William was handsome and dark-skinned with big, brown, expressive eyes. He was so good at his work that he was hired out to work for other cabinetmakers. Ellen's affection was returned, and, in 1846, Eliza gave the two permission to marry.

Slaves were seldom allowed to choose who they wanted to marry—or really to marry at all. They were not allowed a Christian wedding service or even a legal ceremony. Some Black couples could have a bit of a celebration where together they jumped over a broom laid on the ground. That jump indicated they were now married. This was how Ellen and William got married.

The marriage would have been a happy one had Ellen and William not lived with increasing worry over their future together. William had lost track of both his parents and all his siblings when, in his teen years, his plantation master had decided to sell the entire family to pay off his debts. On that horrible day, the man sold William and each member of his family to separate buyers. William never saw any of his loved ones again. Losing his family deeply affected him forever.

Ellen's situation may have been less dramatic, but she had been taken from her mother at age eleven. Because of the very real threat of a plantation master breaking up enslaved families and selling them—even small children—Ellen and William did not want to become parents while they were still enslaved. Their strongest desire was to raise a family, but only in freedom, without fear of separation.

Ellen and William began quietly imagining together how they could make this happen. Clearly their only option was to escape. But how? When an escapee was caught, he or she would be beaten or maimed or sometimes even killed. Plantation owners made an example of them to the other slaves to maintain order. A slave would have to be willing to give all—possibly even life itself—to be free. Escaping all the way from the very Southern state of Georgia to the North, where Black people could live freely, was especially difficult and dangerous. Some chose instead to go farther south to escape, but that had its own special problems.

Ellen continued her seamstress work in her cottage while William worked in the cabinet shop. They each also worked side jobs and saved any money they earned. All the time, Ellen was thinking about how they could escape. Eventually she put together a creative and daring plan, and she waited for the right time to present it to William.

That time came one evening in their cottage. In whispers, Ellen made her case. Since Ellen appeared to be white, and William's dark complexion identified him clearly as Black, what if Ellen pretended to be white and William pretended to be her slave? She could not travel alone as a white woman with a Black slave. That would draw too much attention. But what if she pretended to be a young gentleman? What if they traveled north in their disguise, completely in the open—by train and by boat? Would this be possible?

This plan meant William would be who William really was—an enslaved young Black man from Georgia. But Ellen would need to pretend to be white, privileged, educated, and male. This scheme went well beyond wearing men's clothes. It would also involve her mannerisms, her speech, and her social skills around white people. It would be an amazing feat of acting all around. Could she do it?

Together they decided that, with God's help, it could work. They began intensely planning and praying. Using scraps and hand-me-downs, the talented Ellen sewed a suit of fine clothes to fit herself for the journey: shirt, vest, trousers, and jacket. She had a slender body that could pass for male if she dressed strategically. But what about her voice? What about her lack of facial hair? What about the fact that she, like most slaves, could not read or write?

William had seen many enslaved men traveling with plantation owners, so he knew how he could help Ellen with her disguise. Besides wearing men's clothes, Ellen would wear a man's neck scarf that covered her throat and much of her lower face. William, her personal "slave," would report that she had been ill and couldn't speak, and in fact they were traveling north for "his master's" medical treatment. She would cut her hair to a man's length and wear a hat. She would also wear men's gloves to cover her feminine hands and eyeglasses to make her even less recognizable.

What if she were required to sign papers? Most people were right-handed, so they decided she would put her right arm in a sling as if it were broken. She would stay as silent as possible, William would explain anything that needed explaining, and he would sign papers for her with an X if necessary.

Think again of the changes Ellen would need to make to disguise herself. She would be a woman pretending to be a man, a slave pretending to be free, an illiterate person pretending to be educated, and an impoverished person pretending to be upper class. It was risky in every single way.

Once the decision was made, the two moved quickly, preparing and gathering the items they'd need to make this happen. They planned to leave four days before Christmas, 1848. Favored slaves—which both Ellen and William were—had some time off at Christmas, so the Crafts took full advantage of that. They left in broad daylight on December 21, 1848, to go north. Most escaping slaves were from states on the border between north and south. An escape from Georgia to a free state meant traveling a much longer distance, which would make it that much harder to keep their secret.

At the train station, Ellen bought their tickets. Since they were so far south, there was a separate train car for slaves, so they had to be apart. Each of them worried as the train waited in the station longer than normal. Had someone noticed them leaving home? Would they be recognized?

William watched the station pedestrians from the slave car and saw a man who knew him—William had worked for the man, making cabinets. Fortunately, William was able to dodge being seen before the train rolled out.

At the same time, Ellen, sitting in a first-class car pretending to be a wealthy young man, kept her face to the window and turned away from inside passengers until the train pulled away from the station. She began to breathe a little easier. Then the passenger next to her spoke to her about what a fine day it was. To Ellen's horror, it was a man from a neighboring plantation. This man knew her. Thinking quickly, Ellen was able to indicate with hand gestures that she was unable to speak. He clearly didn't recognize her, and the trip continued without problems.

Two other times Ellen and William thought they would be found out. When they tried to board a steamship, they learned Ellen was lacking paperwork to show that William was her slave. In those days, abolitionists, the people who fought to stop slavery, were often afoot around train stations and ports in the slave states, finding and encouraging enslaved people to escape north to free states. Consequently, slaveholders needed to show written proof of ownership of any slaves traveling with them.

Fortunately, a man who had been on the train with Ellen happened by. He had been impressed with her and with William, so he stepped in and vouched for them. They boarded the boat.

The next stop was still in the South—Baltimore. At the train station, they had the same problem regarding paperwork. This time, a worker at the station overheard the conversation with the ticket agent. He pointed out to the agent that Ellen was clearly ill and seemed to be in pain, and the kind thing to do was allow the two to board the train. The ticket agent relented.

The final stop was Philadelphia, in the free state of Pennsylvania. Ellen and William were so relieved and grateful upon arrival that they literally wept in the train station. Over four nerve-wracking days, they had traveled by train across Georgia to the port of Savannah, up the coast to Charleston, then booked a boat to Wilmington, North Carolina. Then they switched back to train travel, heading inland through some of Maryland and at last to their destination of Pennsylvania.

They'd finally made it to that city full of citizens ready to help newly escaped slaves. Earlier on the trip, a sympathetic abolitionist had quietly encouraged William to escape once he got to Philadelphia, not knowing that was already William's plan. This stranger gave him an address of someone to contact in Philadelphia. Ellen and William did just that.

Fairly soon, the Crafts moved to Boston, where many good things happened, beginning with the ability to marry each other in a Christian ceremony. They had been denied that when they jumped the broom, and it meant everything to the couple that their union be officially sanctioned by God.

They both learned to read and write. In their new home city, the couple became popular speakers and toured the area telling their story. They were able to earn a living this way and became celebrities of a sort. Their thrilling escape story made them the darlings of the speaker circuit for a time. An artist even drew a portrait of Ellen in her disguise and distributed copies to the audience.

But trouble was not over for the Crafts. In 1850, the United States Congress passed the shameful Fugitive Slave Act. This meant that slaveholders had the right to find their escaped "property" in the north and legally take them back south. Of course, the Crafts' previous owner was determined to get Ellen and William back. They were young, talented, and valuable, so he hired two agents to travel to Boston to hunt them down.

Fortunately, word got to the new friends in Boston that men had come to town looking for the Crafts. Abolitionist friends quickly separated the couple and rotated each of them to safe houses around Boston so that they were never together or in one place for very long. Again, the Crafts were spared. The agents never found them, and soon Ellen and William safely boarded a ship for England, where slavery was no longer legal.

Powerful things happened for the Crafts in the next two decades while they lived in London. First, they were able to have the family they so wanted. They had five children in all, never to be taken from them. Second, the Crafts wrote a book about their escape called *A Thousand Miles to Freedom: The Escape of William and Ellen Craft from Slavery*. Published in 1860 in England, the book was highly popular, and it can still be found today online.

The Crafts were once again the toast of the town, speaking to interested groups and selling their book. They worked together for quite some time. But these were Victorian days, a time when the roles of respectable males and females were very rigid. The popular viewpoint was that men were heroes and women were saved by men. So over time, there was social pressure for William to be viewed as the clear leader of the two. Ellen moved more to the background. Eventually William did the speaking tours while Ellen stayed home and sewed. Audiences sometimes expressed their disappointment at not meeting this brave woman of the great disguise.

While we know that Ellen and William worked together to escape, some of that story changed over time. Scholars today believe that it was Ellen who first came up with the disguise idea, and then William and Ellen collaborated in their escape. They wrote their book together too, but mostly only William's point of view is in the book. Their story changed to say that it had been William's idea for Ellen to disguise herself, that he had to persuade her to do it, and that he heroically led the way. In fact, they were both heroes. But at that time, society did not respect the kind of partnership in a marriage that the Crafts had.

After almost two decades abroad, the Crafts moved back to America. The Civil War was over, and finally slavery had been abolished. The couple moved to the South, where Ellen opened a school to teach reading and writing to freed slaves. But although slavery was over, racial unrest was growing in new ways. Her school was burned down by an angry white mob. Since it was too unsafe to stay there, Ellen and William then moved back to their original home area in Macon, Georgia, where they lived the rest of their days. They led a less dramatic life, certainly, but Ellen remained dedicated to educating those who needed it.

Ellen Craft died in 1891, and William died nine years later. We remember Ellen's strong belief in what ought to be: a person ought to be free and children ought to live without fear of being taken from their families. We remember Ellen's creativity to become free. We remember her strong bond with her husband and the teamwork they exhibited. We remember her courage and faith in the face of absolute danger.

In 1996, Ellen Craft—the young, enslaved woman who daringly escaped and lived to tell about it so eloquently both in speech and in writing—was inducted into the Georgia Women of Achievement Hall of Fame.

LET'S REVIEW

1. There were many reasons for enslaved people to want to escape slavery. What was Ellen's most urgent reason?
2. How did Ellen and William "marry" the first time?
3. What new law caused the Crafts to hurry to England?

LET'S DO MORE

Draw a map of the Crafts' escape route from the plantation in Georgia to Philadelphia. Indicate their mode of travel throughout. You can find more details about that route from their online memoir.

REBECCA LEE CRUMPLER

(1831–1895)

Physician and Author

"I early conceived a liking for, and sought every opportunity to relieve the sufferings of others."

*K*nock. *Knock.*

The teenage girl woke up suddenly. She lifted her head to listen.

Knock, knock, knock . . .

There was someone at the front door. And it was very late at night.

She quietly got out of the bed she shared with her aunt. She peered out a front window, then creaked open the wooden front door of their small house.

A young man looked back at her. A full moon illuminated his dark eyes, blinking hard in barely restrained panic. "Can you get your aunt? My wife's time is come, and she's in a bad way. It's her first . . ."

The girl nodded and ran to shake her aunt awake. Auntie threw on a shawl and hurried to the door. After a brief conversation with the young man, she said, "Go on back to her, Caleb, and when you get there, put a pot of water on to boil. I'll be right along."

The man nodded silently and jogged into the dark.

Auntie donned her dress and a clean apron, then whisked around the front room, gathering her bag of ointments, cloths, and tools. She stopped and looked at her niece, then she cupped the girl's chin in her hand. "Gonna be a new baby in this world tonight, child. You're old enough now. Get dressed—you're coming to help."

This was the first time Auntie had asked her to assist. Her aunt was known all over the Black community in their Pennsylvania town as a healer and a helper. Pennsylvania was not a slave state, but no white doctor would treat Blacks, even though they were not enslaved. Auntie stepped in where she could. Self-taught in the world of medicine, she had become skilled in midwifery (helping women give birth), natural treatments, and some medical procedures. The community trusted her and depended on her as their only doctor.

The girl felt both excitement and a twinge of fear as she quickly dressed. She was aware that childbirth was a dangerous time for a woman. Auntie waited for her at the open door, and without another word, the two hurried on foot into the moonlit night.

By morning, there was indeed a new baby in the world—a healthy boy. His mother had labored long and hard in this birth, but she was going to be all right too. Auntie showed her niece how to gently clean the newborn infant while she prepared his mother for the baby's first feeding.

The teenage girl was in a state of awe over what she had just experienced. She had assisted in the power of birth, helped keep back the threat of death, and gloried in the grace of God, all in a matter of hours.

As she swabbed the newborn with a linen cloth dipped in a basin of warm water, the girl slowly realized something. Today she knew what she wanted to do with her life. It was as clear to her as the water in that basin. She wanted to be like her aunt: available and willing to help people and make them well. She swaddled the baby boy and held him against her chest. *Lord, bless this baby*, the girl prayed silently. *And Lord, help me do your work, like my aunt does.* Then she handed the baby to his mother.

This girl on the brink of womanhood was also on the brink of stepping into a powerful future in medicine. She would become even more than a community healer. And she was ready.

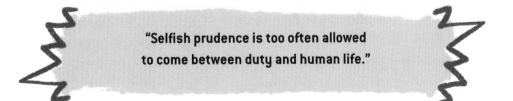

"Selfish prudence is too often allowed to come between duty and human life."

———————

Rebecca Lee Crumpler was born Rebecca Davis in 1831 in the state of Delaware. Although Delaware was technically still a slave state, her parents were free, so she was also free. A high percentage of Delaware Blacks at this time were not enslaved due to the strong moral influence of Quakers and Methodists in this small state, plus the close presence of abolitionists over the northern border.

For some reason, Rebecca was sent to live with an aunt in the neighboring state of Pennsylvania. While we know Rebecca's parents' names—Matilda Webber and Absolum Davis—we don't know the name of the talented and influential aunt who raised her. This unnamed aunt and adoptive mother made a powerful impression on her niece. Rebecca would later write, "Having been reared by a kind aunt in Pennsylvania, whose usefulness with the sick was continually sought, I early conceived a liking for, and sought every opportunity to relieve the sufferings of others."

As a child, Rebecca was noticeably very bright, and her aunt managed to enroll her in an excellent private school. The girl grew up to be tall and straight in stature, and she demonstrated obvious intelligence. She made good on her decision to help others by becoming a nurse.

In 1852, Rebecca married a man named Wyatt Lee, and they moved to Massachusetts, where she used her nursing skills for the next eight years. Rebecca liked her work, but eventually decided she should become a doctor. In those days, one didn't need special training to nurse, but a potential doctor would need to attend medical school. Unfortunately, only a few medical schools admitted women, and none of those admitted Black women.

But Rebecca persevered. She had worked with many different doctors during her years of nursing, and those doctors were impressed with her. Several were willing to write her letters of recommendation to the faculty of New England Female Medical College. This was the first medical school admitting women to train to be a medical doctor (MD). Men in charge argued that women were not intelligent enough to be doctors. And all Blacks were prevented from attending medical school, regardless of gender. But Rebecca was accepted. A local abolitionist offered to pay her tuition, and she was enrolled.

The first women who studied at medical schools were only taught to be better midwives. These were the Victorian days, when some doctors didn't believe it was proper for men to treat women for things like childbirth. Some doctors were even too uncomfortable to use proper medical terms when it came to women's bodies. Those doctors believed the only proper thing to do was train women to doctor other women in areas like pregnancy, childbirth, and women's diseases. But by the time Rebecca enrolled in medical school, that was changing, and she learned doctoring skills for both genders.

During her third year of medical school, Rebecca's husband, Wyatt, died of tuberculosis. They had been married for eleven years, and he had brought a young son to the marriage whom Rebecca considered her own. Unfortunately, the boy had died at age seven. This heartbreaking event may have been one reason Rebecca would become so devoted to helping mothers with the health concerns regarding their babies, their children, and their own health.

A year after the death of her husband, Rebecca received her degree of "Doctress of Medicine" and became the first Black female medical doctor in America. She began practicing in Boston. The following year, Rebecca married again, to Arthur Crumpler, a formerly enslaved man who had gained his freedom and had been living in Canada.

That same year, 1865, the Civil War ended. For a time after the war, exciting things began happening for former slaves in the South. This period of several years was called Reconstruction, when freed Blacks began learning how to read and write, buying their own land, building free communities, and even sometimes holding political office. For a while, there was positive change.

Some Northerners, both Black and white, went south to be a part of the change. Dr. Crumpler was one of them. She moved to the state of Virginia, which was heavily populated with former slaves. She chose to work in the city of Richmond, which was in ruins from the war. She called it "a proper field for real missionary work," and she treated very poor Black people who had no other access to a doctor. Freedom for slaves had changed nothing with Southern white doctors; they still would not treat Black people.

Even though there was a common cause among medical people moving south during Reconstruction, Rebecca experienced an enormous amount of disrespectful behavior from fellow doctors because she was both Black and female. She was sometimes denied hospital privileges as a doctor. She had to fight for the treatments and prescriptions her patients needed. Some doctors—all white males—mocked her, even saying that the MD after her name stood for "Mule Driver," a common occupation of former slaves. But Dr. Crumpler simply continued the work she believed God created her to do. She knew her purpose, and neither racism nor sexism would stop her.

In 1869, the Crumplers returned to Boston and lived on Beacon Hill. Rebecca started a medical practice in their home at 67 Joy Street, treating poor Blacks, often without pay. She especially concentrated on the health of babies, children, and women. She was stunned at how many little ones became seriously ill or even died from illnesses that could have been prevented or successfully treated, and she did her part to change that.

The Crumplers thrived in Boston. They were active members of Twelfth Baptist Church, where Arthur was a trustee. They had a good strong marriage. Their only child, daughter Lizzie Sinclair Crumpler, was born a year into the medical practice, in December 1870. Rebecca had an opinion on the secret to a successful marriage—that a couple should "continue in the careful routine of the courting days." In other words, cherish one another.

Rebecca Lee Crumpler doctored people with dignity and skill until 1880, when she stopped working as much in her clinic so that she could write a book. She suspected people could take care of many health issues at home if they only had a helpful resource, so she wrote one: *A Book of Medical Discourses in Two Parts*, published in 1883. This very readable book was written primarily to women as a guide to their pregnancies, births, babies, and children, and their own health, as well as the health of the males in their lives. In those pages, Rebecca also shared stories about her life experiences and her views regarding health. Her book contains the most personal information available to us about this gifted woman.

As a naturalist as well as a medical doctor, Rebecca was able to convey what she knew and to speak to anxious or suffering people in ways they could understand. She did the same in her writing. Her book was easy to follow and understand. Her directions were specific. She was one of the first in medicine to warn people of the dangers of smoking and tobacco, and she was very ahead of her time with that claim.

If one could read, this was a book one could use. And that was the point. Rebecca knew that many Blacks still had trouble getting proper medical care, so at least they could help themselves in some areas of their family's health. Like many books of the time, this one can be found and read online today.

Rebecca Lee Crumpler lived until 1895, but she was forgotten by the public for many years and was buried in an unmarked grave in Boston. There isn't even an existing photograph of her.

But today Dr. Crumpler is celebrated. The Rebecca Lee Crumpler Society was founded in 1989 to spotlight medicine as a career choice for Black women. Her house on Joy Street became part of the Boston Freedom Trail. And in July 2020, admirers raised funds to place a granite headstone on her grave in Boston's Fairview Cemetery.

Crumpler wrote that what was needed in medicine was "womanly usefulness" and "courageous readiness to do when and wherever duty calls." She practiced medicine, indeed. But she also practiced what she preached in this regard, calling out to Black women to heal others, even in the face of racial and gender prejudice.

Dr. Rebecca Lee Crumpler certainly led the way.

LET'S REVIEW

1. Who raised Rebecca?
2. What degree did Rebecca earn?
3. What was her book about? On what areas did it focus?

LET'S DO MORE

Dr. Crumpler knew she had information to offer, so she wrote a book that would reach more people than she could in person. Are you an expert about something or someone? Could you write about it for others to understand? Could you draw images to help explain it? Write a pamphlet or a short book, or put your knowledge into a short play to perform.

(1848–1912)

Civil War Army Nurse and Teacher

"My services were given at all times for the comfort of these men. . . .
I assisted in caring for the sick and injured comrades."

She came from a line of enslaved yet strong women. One grandmother lived to be a hundred years old, and one great-great-grandmother lived to be 120 years old. Another grandmother somehow gained her freedom during slavery and could even read and write. That's the grandmother who helped raise this child.

At seven years of age, the girl was sent from her birthplace plantation to live with her widowed grandmother in Savannah, Georgia. No one knows why the plantation master allowed a slave child to move off his plantation, but that's what happened. The child who had been growing up in the islands off Georgia's coast now lived in the bustling seaside town of Savannah.

Enslaved people were not allowed to read or write in Georgia in the early 1800s. It was barred by law. But her grandmother in Savannah was literate, and she taught other Black people how to read and write in secret. So the child attended her grandmother's secret school for slaves taught by Black teachers. Somehow this school managed to function, as people say, "hidden in plain sight."

Eventually the child attended two schools. She was taught to hide her books by wrapping them in cast-off newspaper. These were not thick books, so she nestled them in a straw basket, the Black female's "pocketbook" of the times. Sometimes she tucked in other things—a biscuit, or maybe a yarn doll—to keep her basket looking perfectly harmless. The little girl moved seamlessly through the streets and alleys of Savannah to get to and from school. There she learned to read and write and do arithmetic. She quickly understood the beauty of how words came to life on paper, and she learned so easily that her teachers soon had no more to teach her.

She carried her secret reading skills in her child's heart until the day came when, while in her young teen years, she had the chance to teach others how to read and write. And she did all this against a terrifying background.

Because at the same time this young teen became a teacher, she also became a practicing nurse, using her healing arts day and night on the sick and injured.

In an active war zone.

———

She was born Susan Ann Baker in the Sea Islands off the coasts of South Carolina and Georgia in 1848. Her parents were enslaved, and she was their firstborn child. When Susie was seven years old, she was sent to Savannah, Georgia, to live with her grandmother, a widow named Dolly. The reasons she moved there and why such movement was allowed for a child slave are not known.

Grandmother Dolly was a free woman. She could read and write, and she could teach. This was highly rare among Black slaves prior to

"It seems strange how our aversion to seeing suffering is overcome in war . . . and instead of turning away, how we hurry to assist in alleviating their pain, bind up their wounds, and press cool water to their parched lips, with feelings only of sympathy and pity."

the Civil War. Not only was it rare, it was risky. Educating slaves was against the law.

But Grandmother Dolly had a secret school where she taught her granddaughter and other Black children how to read and write. A second secret school in town provided further teaching for the children. This was dangerous for all. The children were taught to flow from the street into the building one by one and quietly. The neighbors most likely thought the children were being taught trade skills in those buildings.

Susie learned how to hide her books and be secretive about her daily life—a life not in the least ordinary. And it was worth it to her. She soaked in her education. But she also learned how to live with risk.

After her teachers felt they had no more to teach Susie, she stopped school for a while. Then a white playmate named Katie, who lived nearby, stepped in. Katie attended a convent for schooling by day, and she offered to give lessons to Susie in secret as long as Susie would not tell Katie's father. Susie agreed, and every night for four months Katie taught Susie what she was learning in her school. At some point, Katie was sent to live in the convent, and Susie never heard from her again.

When Susie was thirteen, the Civil War broke out. Confederate troops were in nearby Fort Pulaski. Within a year, Susie's uncle spirited her and his own children onto a federal gunboat, commanded by the Union Army, in the waters near Fort Pulaski. It's unknown where her parents, Dolly, or her younger siblings were, because she went without them.

Once again, Susie skirted danger as she and thousands of other Black enslaved refugees sought safety so close to Fort Pulaski. She was then moved to one of the South Carolina Sea Islands, and she became attached to the first Black regiment in the US Army: the First South

Carolina Volunteers. This move not only provided safety for Susie and the others but also afforded them their freedom. Since the Union troops were fighting against slavery, Susie was now a free American citizen.

While living with this unit and traveling with them, Susie worked for the troops. She began as a laundress, scrubbing out horrific blood-stains besides cleaning everyday dirty laundry. She also became the unit's cook. But word got around about her literacy, and the unit's white abolitionist colonel, Thomas Wentworth Higginson, called for a meeting with Susie.

Higginson asked Susie if it was true that she could read and write. She said it was true. He asked her to write some things down, apparently to test her. As they chatted, he was further impressed with this young woman. He had never met an educated Black person before, he told her. He asked if she would teach the men how to read. She said yes.

So at age fourteen, Susie became a teacher to the troops and their children. Since this was a Black division of many former slaves, it's likely that none of the troops could read until Susie taught them. She continued to cook and do laundry while teaching hundreds of adults and children how to read and write. Colonel Higginson, clearly impressed, wrote to an associate that his men's "love of the spelling book is perfectly inexhaustible."

Susie had a lot of responsibility helping to keep the troops fed and clothed and now also educating them, all in an active war zone, and she grew up quickly. As battles waged on in earnest, it soon became clear that nurses were needed. Now Susie chose to become a nurse for the unit, which made her the first Black female to be a war nurse in America.

Nursing in those days did not require education or official training. It was an on-the-job training situation, and Susie got plenty of that with the injuries and the illnesses of an army unit. Her sense of compassion and her ability to work tirelessly made her an excellent war nurse. While she still kept the men fed and their clothes clean, Susie had to let teaching go by the wayside for a while in favor of nursing. She was needed for more life-and-death matters.

War injuries were brutal, and Susie saw more horrors than she cared to see. But she was resilient. She tended to the sick as well as the wounded. Smallpox, malaria, measles, and cholera all visited the camp and could be deadly. When it came to smallpox, even in those days there was a vaccine, which Susie had received in time. The rest of the diseases she also treated without fear.

Once, several sick men asked Susie for soup. Supplies were low right then, and she had nothing with which to make soup. She rummaged through supplies and gathered some cans of condensed milk. She then foraged outdoors and found turtle eggs. Even though she had never worked with turtle eggs before (they are not poultry, so they don't cook the same way as other eggs), she managed to make a custard with the milk and eggs. It was a success. The men were so happy to eat something so tasty and easy on their stomachs.

When Susie was fourteen, she did another momentous thing—she married a member of the unit, Sergeant Edward King. The two remained together, moving from base to base, until the war was over. While this was certainly a young age at which to marry, it was not that unusual for the place or time.

Susie and Edward's marriage gave each of them a close family member to love and cherish during these difficult times. But they were also still teenagers together at a time that was both dangerous and exciting for young people, and, more importantly, their life together was full of purpose. They were part of a momentous time in history—protecting fellow Black people, fighting for freedom, and working for a future for Black Americans. Edward fought in the battles, of course. But Susie did all the necessary work to keep the troops alive and well. She also learned how to handle and shoot a musket. She cleaned and assembled firearms for the unit, a task she liked.

While war time is a horrible time, the Kings found happiness together. But the unit itself also found happiness wherever it could. One day a colonel brought a skinny stray pig to the unit. The drummer boys took the pig under their care, nursed him back to health, and taught "Piggie" tricks. By the end of the war, he could even march in time with the drummer boys. This was tolerated because it undoubtedly increased troop morale. Piggie was everyone's pet.

After the war ended, the Kings moved to Savannah. Susie set aside nursing and went back to teaching. She opened a private school for the children of free Blacks at a time when such opportunities were growing in the South, and she hoped to teach more. Edward became a longshoreman, unloading ships at the docks.

Susie soon discovered she was pregnant, which was wonderful news. But unfortunately, Edward had an accident at the docks that killed him. A few months later, as a young widow, Susie gave birth to their son. The school closed, and she became a domestic servant for a few years to support the baby and herself.

Lots of movement in the country was happening for many years after the war. Two different times, Susie found herself in shipwrecks from her travels, struggling in deep waters waiting to be rescued. Even after living through slavery and warfare, she still had dangers in her life.

A few years after Edward died, Susie and her son moved to Boston. This was a better place at the time to be a free Black person and to raise her son, Susie felt. She had a good life there and married again in 1879 to

Russell Taylor. She then dedicated her time to working with a national organization for female Civil War veterans called Women's Relief Corps.

The years passed, and Susie became a widow again. Then sadly, Susie's adult son, who was living in Shreveport, Louisiana, became very ill. She took the long journey by train from Boston to Shreveport with plans to take her son to Boston and nurse him back to health, something she certainly knew how to do well. But she had no idea the scope of racial problems going on in the Deep South. After days of suffering indignities as a Black woman traveling alone, she arrived at her destination to find her son near death. When she tried to book the trip back to Boston, she discovered that no train would sell her a berth because her son was Black, and he was too ill to travel by other means. She stayed with him until he died in Shreveport.

Susie returned to Boston and spent the rest of her life there. In 1902, she wrote and published a memoir of her wartime nursing experiences—the only Black woman to do so. This fascinating book, *Reminiscences of My Life in Camp with the 33d United States Colored Troops Late 1st S.C. Volunteers*, can be found online.

Susie King Taylor died in 1912 in Boston and is buried in Mt. Hope Cemetery. She was sixty-four. She packed a lot of meaningful work into those years. Because of her race, she was never officially credited by the government as being a military nurse. She would forever be known as their "laundress." And because of her race, she was never paid for her work during the war.

But we know how much more she offered, because she left a marvelous account of it all in her memoir. In that book, Colonel C. T. Trowbridge wrote a foreword acknowledging Susie's fine work as a nurse during the war. He also lamented that the government labeled her only as a laundress and paid her no pension.

Susie King Taylor—selfless military nurse, brilliant teacher, and thrilling memoirist—was inducted into the Georgia Women of Achievement Hall of Fame in 2018 for her many contributions to her fellow citizens.

LET'S REVIEW

1. Why did Susie have to learn to read in secret? How did she move books around?
2. How did Susie become free?
3. What jobs did she have during her time with the Army?

LET'S DO MORE

Your soldiers are sick and hungry. What can you feed them that will nourish them? How will you make it? Use anything in the kitchen, but no fast food allowed!

MADAM C.J. WALKER

(1867–1919)

Entrepreneur and Self-Made Millionaire

*"I had to make my own living and my own opportunity.
But I made it."*

She was born on a damp, chilly morning in her parents' tiny cabin. Of course, the birth of a new baby was always a happy thing to be celebrated. But the celebration was even greater because this was the first baby in her family to be born in freedom. For generations, her family members had been enslaved. They had been released from that bondage only a few years before. Now, today, there was a December baby about to embark into the New Year and a newer world. What a glorious Christmas present!

She grew to be a sturdy, healthy little girl, even though sufficient food and creature comforts were hard to come by. Freedom was a powerful thing, but it did not feed anyone. Only work did that. The child watched her parents work hard, and she learned by example to do the same.

On Sundays, things could slow down a little. Since slavery had ended, Blacks could now openly attend church. On that one day a week, before church, Momma would sit cross-legged on the cabin's dirt floor and pull her little girl close to her. This was the day when the child's hair would be braided.

There were no grooming utensils in the world of the enslaved or the former enslaved, not even a comb, for many years to come. Grooming oneself had never been allowed under slavery. The best women could do with their hair was keep it short or groom it when there was a little downtime, usually on Sundays.

On that day, Black women often borrowed the big carding combs used to comb sheep's wool. These carding combs were not clean and could not be made clean since there was no soap available to slaves for personal hygiene. Black women used the sheep combs with a mixture of butter, bacon grease, and kerosene to detangle their hair, and it did the job.

No matter how they fixed their hair, however, Black women were expected to cover it with a scarf in public. During slavery, that was a rule and, in some states, even the law. After slavery ended, rural Southern Black women continued to wrap their heads in cloth for many decades.

The child's mother may have used the sheep-carding combs on her own hair, but for her little girl, Momma used her fingers. She unwrapped and untwisted her daughter's braids and ran long, lightly greased fingers through her hair until everything was smooth. There was no shampoo in those days, so Momma simply braided her daughter's hair again, also weaving in long strips of cloth to further secure her work. She braided tightly, because there would be no time for her to fix things during the days of backbreaking work. Only on Sundays.

The child grew up with this Sunday ritual in her early years. She would relax against her mother's folded legs, and even when Momma pulled her hair too tightly, the child didn't mind. It felt secure. It felt fine because Momma was in charge.

Too soon the little girl was working in fields herself. And it looked like she would have the same life of dismal poverty as all her people had.

But this child was not destined for the fields. And although she did laundry work for many years, she wasn't destined to do that either. Who could know these things? And who could know how those

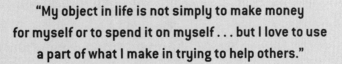

"My object in life is not simply to make money for myself or to spend it on myself . . . but I love to use a part of what I make in trying to help others."

Sunday braiding sessions would come back to mind down the road and help change her life?

Nobody could imagine how successful this child was going to be when she grew up. Or how much she was going to help and lead other Black women—in more ways than one.

———

Sarah Breedlove was born near Delta, Louisiana, two days before Christmas in 1867. She was the youngest of Owen and Minerva Breedlove's six children but the first to be born in freedom after the signing of the Emancipation Proclamation, which freed Southern slaves. For her early childhood years, she grew up in the loving circle of her parents, her four older brothers, and her older sister.

Life was extremely difficult in the Breedloves' world, as it was for all Blacks in Louisiana. Slavery was over, but many things did not change in daily life. For one thing, Black children could not attend school. Sarah and her siblings, even at their tender ages, worked in the cotton fields alongside their parents.

These were happy times at home, though. Sarah was loved and protected by her parents. When she wasn't working, she and her best friend liked to catch crawfish in the nearby bayou. And they sat together at Pollard Church on Sundays, which was always enjoyable.

For a time, Pollard Church was able to offer reading classes. A northern missionary opened a Sunday school class there for former slaves and their families to learn to read, and Sarah attended that class. She was only able to attend for three months, but it was enough for her to learn to read. She always wished she could have attended longer than three months. Later in her life, she would do something about that for others who needed an education.

When Sarah was six, her mother died of a fever from a cholera outbreak. One year later, her father died of the same kind of fever. At age seven, Sarah was an orphan. Relatives pitched in to help raise the younger Breedlove children, and then, at age ten, Sarah moved to Vicksburg, Mississippi, to live with her now-married sister, Louvenia.

The rest of Sarah's childhood was very lonely. She had started life in a home where she felt safe and loved, but too quickly, that turned. Living with her sister should have been a safe and loving time. But Louvenia's husband, Jesse, was cruel. He was verbally abusive and violent. He complained about having Sarah in his house and threatened her in several ways. He insisted that she, at age ten, hire out as a laundress, someone who washed and ironed white people's laundry.

Sarah had picked cotton as a youngster. But laundry was a very different thing altogether. In these days in the late 1800s, before many people had running water in their homes, a laundress like Sarah would pump well water from an outside pump and fill huge pots of it in the yard. She boiled the laundry in the water with lye soap, stirring it with a stick. Then she would wring it all out and pin the wet, heavy pieces of laundry to clotheslines.

This was done in all kinds of weather except extreme rain. When the laundry was almost dry, Sarah would iron it with a flatiron—a heavy, triangular shaped iron heated on the stove. She had to learn not to scorch the laundry with such a hot iron. This was hard work for a grown woman, much less a ten-year-old child. But Sarah did it. Whatever money she made, she gave to Jesse and Louvenia.

A few years later, Sarah figured out how to change her situation. At the young age of fourteen, she married Moses McWilliam to get away from her abusive brother-in-law. Fortunately, Moses was a good man, and Sarah felt safe and fairly content, especially when, four years later, she gave birth to a daughter. They named her Lelia, and she would be Sarah's only child. Only one year after Lelia's birth, Moses died suddenly. There is no record as to how this young man died.

Now Sarah was alone with a baby. Life became harder. Her older brothers had moved to St. Louis, Missouri, and together they owned a successful barbershop, so Sarah decided to join them. This was before the Great Migration of Southern Black people to the north, so she was being especially adventurous, putting baby Lelia and herself on a train in hopes of a better life.

They did indeed have a better life in St. Louis. Her brothers were an anchoring point for Sarah, and she joined a handsome downtown church a block from the barbershop, St. Paul's African Methodist Episcopal Church. There she met Black women from different walks of life. She had been raised with mostly former slaves who, in their new freedom, were trying to carve lives for themselves in the middle of a world that did not want to change how it treated Black people. The post–Civil War South was still dangerous to Blacks, and that continued for decades.

In St. Louis, however, there were close-knit neighborhoods of Blacks supporting one another in every way. Black people lived in houses, not shacks. They owned businesses. Their children went to school. People felt free to walk around, socialize, and enjoy life. Everyone still worked hard, but there was more to show for that hard work.

St. Paul's had a population of Black women who had education and poise. Sarah paid attention to how they acted, looked, and sounded. She watched how the grand ladies of the church spoke and carried themselves, and she followed their example.

The church believed the Bible instructed them to care for widows and children, so Sarah and little Lelia were supported in many ways.

Thanks to the fine ladies at St. Paul's, Lelia received an education and sometimes even meals when laundry work didn't make ends meet. Sarah was encouraged by this. She also began to give back, and, as she became more stable financially, she helped others out where she could.

Sarah was no longer a fieldworker, but she was still doing hard domestic work. Years later Sarah would remember a conversation she had with herself. "I was at my washtubs one morning with a heavy wash before me," she reported. "As I bent over the washboard and looked at my arms buried in soap suds, I said to myself, 'What are you going to do when you grow old and your back gets stiff? Who is going to take care of your little girl?'" That self-prompting got Sarah to move from doing laundry in St. Louis to working as a housekeeper and cook. She also worked in her brothers' barbershop.

Influenced by her brothers, Sarah began learning about hair care. She started using hair products for Black women made by the Poro Company, and then she became a saleswoman for that company. This was an empowering time for Sarah, who saw herself moving into a whole new world once she stopped doing laundry. She also was forming an expertise in Black women's hair.

Black women's hair has a history much longer than America's history. Most enslaved people had been kidnapped from their homes near the western coast of Africa. They were stolen from longtime, sophisticated cultures. If they managed to survive the horrific ocean trip to America, they were put on an auctioneer's block and sold like livestock. One way of dehumanizing them was to shave their heads, both men and women alike. Black women were then made to cover their shorn heads.

In western Africa, hair was honored. One could tell from another's hairstyle what tribe the person was from and sometimes that person's social status. African women used special combs and mixtures of fragrant herbs and natural oils to groom their hair. They grew their hair long and created elaborate hairstyles. An online search for African women's hairstyles shows these. That was one of many vibrant traditions torn away from Africans—a sense of identity that went along with their hair.

After a few generations of enslavement, most of that hair history was lost. Black people in America—especially women—were shown so much disrespect because of their tight curl that they lived in head wraps. Many began to view their natural, God-given hair only as a problem to be dealt with. At the same time, that lack of basic haircare and hygiene caused unhealthy scalps. Because of this, plus poor nutrition, many Black women's hair fell out in patches. They continued to wear the head wrap.

After the Civil War until the early twentieth century, Black women were not seen in public much other than walking to and from work. They worked all the time, and their paying work involved being indoors cleaning and cooking, or boiling laundry in their yards. That would start changing in Sarah's lifetime. Black women were more out and about, not just indoors. Thousands of women moved north for a less subservient lifestyle, and they discovered communities of other Black people who socialized outside the home.

Consequently, women's outer appearances changed once they were being seen by others. Of course they would shed the head wrap that belonged to someone in servitude and want to show their glorious hair. If their hair was falling out or otherwise unhealthy, that was a problem.

Like Black men frequented barbershops, soon Black women enjoyed frequenting Black beauty parlors, as they were called. Black women were getting their hair treated and styled, but they were also socializing and sharing ideas. Beauty parlors became a safe place for Black women. Sarah must have remembered those Sunday sessions of hair braiding with Momma when she discovered beauty shops. Hair seemed to bring women and girls together.

Sarah was one of the unfortunate women whose hair fell out. It was very upsetting. Using the Poro product helped, but Sarah began to pray for something better. Then one night she had a dream. In the dream, an African man showed her how to mix a solution to repair her hair and scalp. When she woke up, she clearly remembered the dream and believed it was sent by God, and she went about finding the many ingredients.

Some ingredients she recognized from the Poro product, but there were other ingredients that were new to Sarah. She mixed the solution in a pot over her kitchen stove, used it—and it worked. Her hair came back and grew in a healthy way. After watching these results, Sarah began sharing her concoction with other women to see if it helped their hair too.

During this time, Sarah met Charles Joseph (C. J.) Walker, a handsome man who worked in a variety of positions in Black newspapers. He was educated and well dressed, and they found they shared a lot of the same goals in life. They were married, and now Sarah went by Mrs. C. J. Walker.

Sarah's hair was growing nice and lush, and so was the hair of many women she shared her product with. She came to believe other women would want it. She and her husband discussed the situation, and a business was born. She called her product *Madam Walker's Wonderful Hair Grower*. There were other Black haircare products out there, so her idea was not new, but her formula and her story were unique. Sarah understood the concept of marketing. She knew it was good to share her story, and she also distinguished her product from others by adding the French title "Madam" to her name. This was her way of notching up the sophistication level. She was called Madam C. J. Walker for the rest of her life.

A successful hair formula was just the beginning for Sarah's new business. She had a larger vision for what was to come, and she worked hard to make it happen. She eventually would have many products, not just the hair-growing formula. Soon she would sell face powders, shampoo, skin creams, pomade for men, and her version of the hot comb. Since there were other companies making products for the same market, Sarah began having her image included on every package of product. At a quick glance, the customer could trust the product because Madam's picture was on it. This was true even for women who could not read well.

Sarah's success had its critics. There was a standard of beauty in America that was strictly Caucasian. That caused some Black women to want to straighten their hair and lighten their skin. An activist named Nannie Helen Burroughs was widely quoted as saying, "What every woman who bleaches and straightens out needs is not her appearance changed but her mind." So some critics felt Sarah was helping Black women look as white as they could by selling them a product that relaxed their hair.

But Sarah flatly denied this. She never tried to look white, and she only wanted women to have a healthy scalp, hair, and skin, and to look like their natural selves. She wanted them to feel confident enough to go out in the world and do what they needed and wanted to do with their lives. She celebrated Black women's hair, and she was adamant that her goal was to provide Black women access to their own personal beauty and personal power. It seems she was onto something, because business boomed.

While the products were good, Sarah's company really grew when she hired Black women to sell them door-to-door. They were called

Walker Agents, and eventually there would be forty thousand of them. This kind of direct selling of products not available in stores predates companies like Avon. Sarah trained her saleswomen to know all there was to know about the products—and of course, they used the products themselves. They dressed in black skirts and crisp white blouses, carried black briefcases, and hit the sidewalks, meeting each customer right in her home.

What a success this was. Sarah paid her Walker Agents well and provided bonuses. She wanted Black women to have a choice in their employment. She wanted them not to have to work in service positions for white people if they didn't want to. She remembered what it was like, working so hard for very little money or respect. Now Black women could earn a living doing something they liked. Interviews with some of the Walker Agents exist online. Working as a Walker Agent offered independence, a good living, and dignity. And there was something else these women weren't used to: the work was enjoyable.

As the business grew, there were other job opportunities for Black women who didn't want to be in sales. Fairly early, Sarah opened a warehouse in Indianapolis where workers made the product, packaged it, and shipped it. Most of those employees were Black women. She opened schools where women employees could train beauticians in the use of Walker hair and skin products. She employed Black women all over America and in the Caribbean and Central America.

By 1915, Sarah—Madam C. J. Walker—became America's first self-made female millionaire, Black or white. With that wealth came giving back to others. Sarah donated lots of money to causes she believed in—causes that would help Black people increase their education, safety, and social status. She donated to the arts. She also gave freely to her friends.

Sarah developed plans for a building in Indianapolis to be a full-service location for both the business and the Black community. She designed a building that was several stories high and took up a whole block. The style of the building was called "flatiron." This was the triangular shape that accommodated diagonal streets in cities. Many cities had and still have buildings of this style.

Her plans to build were put on hold as Sarah's health began to fail. She was troubled with hypertension, which had led to some kidney failure, and her doctor wanted her to slow down. But Sarah had never slowed down in her life. Maybe she didn't know how. Eventually her busy lifestyle took its toll, and she died at age fifty-one.

Sarah's daughter, Lelia, took over the company upon her mother's death. According to Sarah's will, two-thirds of her vast estate went to charity. The company went to daughter Lelia, and she led the operations, following her mother's wish that the company always be headed by a woman.

Lelia oversaw the construction of the Walker Building in Indianapolis. She built it according to her mother's plans, and it was as grand as Sarah had hoped it would be. It was the national headquarters of the Madam C. J. Walker Manufacturing Company, and product was produced and packaged in the huge flatiron building. Besides the company offices, the Walker Building housed a barbershop, beauty shop, coffeeshop, ballroom, venues for live music, and a palatial movie theater, the first in Indianapolis to cater to Black customers. The Walker Building became an extraordinary gathering place for Black people in Indianapolis. The building still stands today as a National Historic Landmark.

Sarah Breedlove-turned-Madam C. J. Walker made her mark in the world, and it wasn't just that she was rich. She used what she had to help others. Imagine starting out as an orphan doing laundry for money and winding up in a place to help others in so many ways. Her vast philanthropy is rarely equaled even today. Imagine the thousands of women whose lives were changed by working at the Walker Company. Their experiences forever impacted how Black women could work and live.

Like so many businesses, the Madam C. J. Walker Manufacturing Company did not survive the Great Depression. Some of Madam C. J. Walker's products, however, live on today at the Sephora company, though these products no longer carry Madam's image on them.

But we can still see her image in all its glory on an American stamp released in 1998. The black-and-white photo shows the gracious, brilliant Madam C. J. Walker with her smooth skin and textured hair and her serene, Mona Lisa gaze. Fortunately, we'll always be able to see that image and enjoy the legacy of this great woman.

LET'S REVIEW

1. What occupations did Sarah have before forming her own company?
2. Why did Sarah's hair fall out?
3. Why did Sarah put her own image on all her products?

LET'S DO MORE

Research African women's hair in the library or online. Can you fix your hair or someone else's to look like some of these coifs? If you are someone who draws, make some sketches of the intricate styles. Also note the beautiful head coverings. Can you make any yourself and learn to wrap them around your head?

BESSIE COLEMAN

(1892–1926)

Pilot

"I made my mind up to try. I tried and was successful."

The child dragged her heavy burlap sack of cotton down the dirt row in the hot sun. It was hard to believe something as fluffy as a cotton boll could add up to be so much weight to move around. The field was full of workers, many from her own family. She was not the only child present.

In rural Texas, as the 1800s rolled into the 1900s, life was undeniably difficult for Black sharecropper families. Children worked the fields alongside adults, and this child understood that her labors helped feed her many brothers and sisters. Even at a young age, she understood how crops in the field turned into food on the table and that, as a picker, she was part of that production chain.

She was a bright child who excelled in math and loved to read. She wished she could be in school more often, but Southern schools were segregated, and schools for Black children were only open a few months per year. White educators and lawmakers did not consider it important to educate Black children, so school was not open for Black children during picking season. Then, Black children worked in the fields instead of going to school.

As the child stopped to change rows, she straightened up and adjusted the straw hat she wore to ward off sun sickness. She heard the familiar sound of a mockingbird from the tree line. She lifted her face to watch it break away from the foliage and soar overhead. She stood still for a moment. Wouldn't it be something to be able to fly way up in the sky like that, with the birds? Were there angels up there too?

Well, she was on the ground in this cotton field, not in the air, and that's just how it was.

Still, wouldn't it be something?

Elizabeth "Bessie" Coleman was born in her family's dirt-floor cabin near Waxahachie, Texas, in 1892. Her mother, Susan Coleman, was Black, and her father, George Coleman, was Black and one-quarter Cherokee. Neither parent could read or write. Bessie was the tenth of thirteen children, though only nine of them survived to adulthood—a sad statistic that was not unusual for the time and place due to devastating poverty.

This was a time in America of great industry and exciting new inventions. A new century was approaching, and the world felt the excitement of that. But Bessie knew nothing about this. Her young life was spent working the cotton fields, attending the local church, and going to school when she could. Her prospects as a Black child in Texas were dim. Her future seemed already laid out—a future of hard work and poverty.

But Bessie had dreams that went beyond her early environment. Once she finished the schooling available to her, she set her sights on college. This alone showed both imagination and extraordinary drive for a girl brought up picking cotton at the turn of the century. She managed to work and save enough money to attend college in Langston, Oklahoma, for one term. Accomplishing that was highly unusual, given her status at the time. Unfortunately, she had to drop out when her funds ran out. Bessie moved home, took a job as a laundress, and pondered her future.

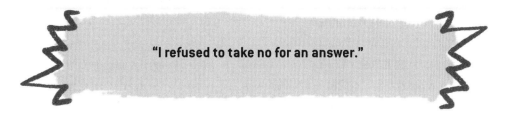

"I refused to take no for an answer."

Between the years 1910 and 1970, the Great Migration was happening, a time when millions of Black people in the American South moved north for better jobs and freer lives. In 1913, at age twenty-one, Bessie joined them and moved to Chicago to live with her two older brothers, John and Walter. The bustling city of Chicago was quite a change from the cotton fields of Texas, and Bessie loved it. She worked as a manicurist in the White Sox Barber Shop, and she saved her money—for what? She wasn't sure, but it seemed in Chicago the whole world was opening to her. She worked, she watched, and she waited.

The end of World War I was the beginning of a shift in Bessie's world. John and Walter fought in Europe as part of an all-Black military division. They returned and regaled her with stories of France. So did many Black customers in the barbershop. In addition to that, they all talked about how well they were treated as Black men by the Europeans. John and Walter also told Bessie stories about the bravery of French women, who they said fought alongside the men at war. These stories made an impression on Bessie.

In those days, many people got their news from daily newspapers and from the movie theater "newsreels," films that showed world events of the day. This included footage of the thrilling new industry of flying. On the screen, Bessie watched these aviators, in particular the daring escapades of Harriet Quimby, an American who was the first female to fly across the English Channel.

Now Bessie had a dream. She told her brothers she was going to learn to fly. They laughed.

But Bessie wasn't laughing. Although this was a few years before the famous Amelia Earhart hit the flying scene, Bessie was determined she would learn to fly, and she proceeded to apply to flight schools around the country. She was rejected by all of them. Why? Because she was Black.

Bessie was not a stranger to difficulties, so when no flight schools would train her because of her race, she simply continued to save her money and wait for an opportunity to come along. Her brothers called her crazy, but Bessie had always loved a challenge. When she finally found a flight school in France that would teach her, a Black woman, she took a second job in a chili house to add to her manicurist's wages so she could pay for this next step in her life.

Bessie appealed to Robert Abbott, owner of a popular newspaper for Black readers called the *Chicago Defender*. Bessie felt the world should see what she was seeing: flight was the future, and Black people needed to get involved in that future. Abbott was impressed by her. He published her views. This led some readers to become her sponsors and help Bessie finance this dream of flying.

For the next year, Bessie went to language school in Chicago. She was already a whiz at math, so when she became fluent enough in the French language to study aerodynamics, she made her move. The country girl from Texas took a train from Chicago to New York City, boarded a steamship, and sailed to France.

In flight school, Bessie found she was not treated differently because she was Black. The teachers and students at the school simply respected her as one of them—someone who wanted to fly. She realized those war veterans in the Chicago barbershop were right. French people cared about who you were, not your race. It was a powerful experience.

On June 15, 1921, Bessie finished her study and training at the Fédération Aéronautique Internationale and became the first Black American—and the first Native American—to earn an international pilot's license. She returned to the States to get more in-the-air training, but still nobody would work with a Black woman. She went back to France and trained with ace flyers there for the next two years to perfect her skills.

Upon returning to the States this time, Bessie started flying for the public and gained almost instant fame. The press named her "Queen Bess" and celebrated her as a world-class stunt pilot. People watched her on newsreels and saw her in the daily newspapers. Americans began to recognize the good-looking young woman with a heart-shaped face dressed in her jaunty pilot's suit, always with a pilot's signature white silk scarf tied around her neck.

In those early days of flying, pilots were known for performing daring acts in the air. That was also the case with Bessie. Flying was new enough that pilots couldn't yet earn a living carrying passengers, so they did amazing things in the air and hoped to get paid for that. Most of them, like Bessie, also wanted to advance this fledgling industry in the public's imagination. She especially wanted to encourage Black Americans to live their dreams—including dreams of flying.

Airplanes then did not have enclosed cabins. Pilots flew in the open air, and they wore goggles because of the air blasting into the open cockpit. Planes were made of light materials, which could make controlling them tricky.

Nevertheless, these pioneer pilots flew upside down, under bridges, and through wooden buildings (activities called "barnstorming") in those open cockpits. Even more unbelievably, they climbed out of that airborne cockpit to perform—walking on the wing, hanging from the wheel, climbing up poles, and other stunts. Historic footage is available online that clearly demonstrates how dangerous this was.

These pilots had to be part athlete, part mathematician, and part acrobat to be successful. And brave. Bessie was all of those. She was of average height and build, but she was strong. She had to be physically fit with good stamina and a strong sense of balance to do the kind of activities aviators of the day performed. She needed a healthy respect for what her body could do in the air while moving. She could harbor no fear of heights. She had to be able to mathematically gauge some of her stunts—like, for example, exactly how much space she had and when to duck while standing on the wing of a plane flying under a bridge (this can be seen online).

Many pilots, including Bessie, also became paid public speakers, telling audiences about the world of flight and sharing their thrilling experiences. While airshows were promoted for entertainment, pilots also wanted the world to be informed about this fledgling industry and to join in the experience.

Bessie earned some of her living giving aviation lectures. People flocked to hear this young "aviatrix," as women aviators were termed, speak about her life in the air. She was liberally quoted by the press, saying things such as "You've never lived till you've flown," "You can fly high, just like me," and "The air is the only place free from prejudices."

She was also an activist. She was a Black American who had tasted the dignity of being treated well in France. She had no patience now for Jim Crow—American laws that segregated races and held Blacks back. If an airshow or a speaking venue would not let Black people enter through the front entrance, she simply would not perform or give speeches there. She was highly regarded for taking that stand.

In the 1920s, Bessie made new friends while on a speaking tour in Orlando, Florida. Reverend Hezakiah Hill and his wife, Viola, invited her to stay with them for a time in their parsonage, and she became very close to the couple and their church congregation. The Hills encouraged her to live nearby and treated her like a daughter. Bessie became so close to her new "family" that when she decided to open a beauty shop to help finance a new plane, she located it near them in Orlando.

In 1923, Bessie bought her new plane in San Diego, California. While flying to Los Angeles, the plane had engine failure and crashed. She was found unconscious. Bessie remained in the hospital for the next three months, recovering from a broken leg, several broken ribs, and a bruised and beaten face. Her spirit, however, was anything but broken. She let the press know that this was only a bump—that people should not view flying as unsafe. She'd survived just fine. Queen Bess would be back.

After her time in the hospital, Bessie embarked on a long recovery. It took two years, and while she did not exactly bounce back, she did get well. Then she went back to pouring herself into her work. In 1925 Bessie went on a barnstorming tour on her way back to Florida, putting on thrilling airshows in town after town in America. One stop was her hometown of Waxahachie, Texas, where the townspeople were excited to see their local talent, and her family let her know how proud they were.

Unfortunately, like many pilots of that day, Bessie Coleman died young. Although she died flying, it wasn't a stunt that killed her. She was the passenger in an open cockpit plane flown by a mechanic and pilot named William Willis. He had flown this plane to the Jacksonville, Florida, location where she would be performing. He'd had some problems flying there that required three emergency landings, but all that had been fixed. Bessie's family and friends still felt nervous about the aircraft, but Bessie would not be talked out of performing in the upcoming airshow.

On April 30, 1926, Bessie and William took off for an aircheck to prepare for the next day's performance. She was seated in the open cockpit but not belted in. As she would be using a parachute at her performance the next day, she needed to lean over the front of the aircraft to formulate her plans. But within minutes of takeoff, the plane suddenly flipped over for no apparent reason and went into a spin. Bessie was immediately thrown to her death. The pilot tried valiantly to gain control but could not. The plane quickly spiraled down, and he died also in a fiery crash.

How did this happen? After all the risks Bessie took in her flying career, why would she die this way? Investigators were able to determine that an error on the ground had caused the problem. A wrench had accidentally been left in the engine during the repairs, and it jammed up the mechanism in flight. This caused the plane to flip.

Bessie's body was sent to her adopted hometown of Chicago, where she was buried. Over ten thousand mourners showed up to honor her.

It is normal to hope talented people can live long, productive lives. Bessie lived to only age thirty-four. But her last decade was full of accomplishments that left a strong legacy. Bessie had said, "If I can create a minimum of my plans and desires, there shall be no regrets." She achieved far more than the "minimum." She didn't simply provide entertainment as a pilot. She provided inspiration.

Bessie believed she was part of the beginning stages of what would be a strong industry in the future—flight. She knew pioneers of the air did not live long lives, and she said, "I thought it my duty to risk my life to learn aviation and to encourage flying among men and women of our race, who are so far behind the white race in this modern study." Consequently, when she died she was in the planning stages of her next dream—opening a flight school for students from all walks of life. Bessie had a teacher's spirit, and she wanted to never again see someone Black turned away from training.

In 1929 the Bessie Coleman Aero Club formed to promote aviation among the Black community. Among the many inspired by this organization were the courageous Tuskegee Airmen—the first Black men to fly fighter planes, during World War II. They claimed Bessie Coleman as one of the reasons they existed as a group. For many years, on Queen Bess's birthday, Tuskegee Airmen flew low over Bessie's grave in Chicago and dropped white flowers from the air.

Bessie showed how to move beyond your beginnings—to literally fly over them and into the future. She was the reason we would have Black aviators. And Black astronauts. When Mae Jemison became the first Black female to fly in space, aboard the space shuttle *Endeavor*, she kept a photo tucked in her pocket. It was a picture of Bessie Coleman.

LET'S REVIEW

1. What are some reasons Bessie moved to Chicago?
2. How did early pilots earn a living?
3. What caused the plane to crash in Florida?

LET'S DO MORE

The internet is full of film clips of air flight throughout the last hundred years. Go online and find black-and-white clips of Queen Bess in flight. While you're there, look around for film clips of other barnstormers and daring aviation performers of the same era. What are your thoughts about these performances in such a young industry? Would you be inspired to try such flying?

SELMA BURKE

(1900–1995)

Sculptor

"Art didn't start black or white, it just started."

She was seven years old, a quiet child who watched the world around her with wide, dark eyes. She grew up down the road from a river where she liked to play, sometimes with her nine brothers and sisters, sometimes alone. She loved the feel of the riverbed's white clay in her hands—damp and soft and firm all at the same time. She would dig her fingers deep into that cool clay. The very movement seemed to spark her imagination.

One day she noticed the imprints her fingers made, imprints that did not dissolve easily. She began to play differently in the clay, making things with it—sculpting household objects or realistic forms of small animals. When she realized she could make things with her own hands in this way—solid things that looked like the world around her—it felt so natural. The little girl knew something momentous was happening with the clay at the riverbed, and she would say, many years later, "It was there in 1907 that I discovered me."

At home, her artist grandmother inspired her, referring to what the child did as "art." Her minister father encouraged her. Her practical mother helped steer her path. Consequently, the child's creative spirit was respected and nurtured by those who mattered in her world. Never mind that she was a Black child in the South in a time of horrible inequalities. She would cultivate this God-given artistic talent.

One day the child sculpted a small house from the river clay. But the water got to it and washed it away. When her sister laughed at her predicament, as sisters sometimes do, the child turned to her and said, "One of these days I'm gonna do something with my stuff that you won't laugh at."

Her sister always remembered that. Because the day did indeed arrive when the world saw and respected what her sister created. Many pieces of her art are with us today.

In fact, we see her art every time we spend an American dime.

———————

Selma Hortense Burke was born on New Year's Eve, 1900, in Mooresville, North Carolina, to Reverend Neil Burke and Mary Elizabeth Colfield Burke. Her father was a Methodist minister who also worked as a chef on cruise ships for income. He was often gone on long voyages, and he brought home toys and objects from foreign lands for his ten children.

When it came to art, young Selma's family was unusual. Her grandmother was a painter, and she saw the artistic talent in her grandchild. Selma's father also saw it and encouraged her to continue sculpting. She used the exotic and colorful objects he brought home from his travels as models for sculpting.

The Burke family had inherited many African sculptures and masks from Selma's uncles who had done missionary work in Africa. Eventually those pieces were given to Selma, but in her childhood her mother kept that artwork in the attic. She considered them "graven images" and not something for her Christian child to pay too much attention to. So Selma went up to the attic and studied the pieces. African art was rarely seen in America in the early part of the twentieth century,

"It is very inspiring to release a figure from a piece of stone or wood."

but Selma became well versed in what she could see in the attic. These pieces influenced her artistic direction and opened her mind to sculpting even more.

The Burke children were educated in a one-room schoolhouse in the segregated South, so they were lacking in books and in the amount of time spent in school. But they were rich in family support. Selma's folks were clear that this talented child would be going on to a higher education. Selma intended to be an artist, but her mother strongly encouraged her daughter to become a nurse, believing that art could not provide a living, especially for a Black woman, but nursing could offer steady work and a respectable life.

In 1922 Selma graduated from Slater Industrial and Slater Normal School (later to be called Winston-Salem University) to become a teacher. Then, to please her mother, in 1924 she graduated from St. Agnes Training School for Nurses in Raleigh, North Carolina, becoming a registered nurse.

Shortly after receiving her degrees, Selma married an old friend from childhood, Durant Woodward. Sadly, her husband died one year later of blood poisoning. Selma altered her plans for the future now that she'd lost her husband. In 1929, she left North Carolina and made a big move to New York City.

In New York, Selma worked as a private nurse for an heiress who introduced her to the New York art world. Soon Selma met members of the African American art world in Harlem, a vibrant Black neighborhood in New York City. She decided it was time to concentrate on her own art. She attended Sarah Lawrence College, majoring in art, working as a model in art classes to pay her tuition, and sculpting in her spare hours.

During Selma's time in New York, something called the Harlem Renaissance was in full bloom—a time in the 1920s and 1930s when African

American art, music, dance, literature, and theater were captivating the nation and even the world. That Renaissance was centered in Harlem.

During those years, the circle of artists and writers Selma came to know encouraged her to develop her own artistic vision. As the Great Depression descended on the nation, she not only concentrated on her art but also worked in newly developed government programs such as the Works Progress Administration (WPA) and the Harlem Artists Guild. She taught art appreciation to the youth of New York City. She found she was as much a teacher as she was an artist, and she would teach throughout her life.

Harlem friends now encouraged Selma to move to Paris, where she could develop her own art more fully. Paris was truly the place to go for artists to find their self-expression. And in Paris, American Blacks were treated as well as native Parisians. Selma moved to that beautiful French city and came to know the great artist Henri Matisse. He openly appreciated her work, telling her she had "a big talent." She would count him as a strong influence. He advised her on how to be more honest in her work, advice she would follow throughout her career. During this time, Selma also traveled across Europe for more artistic influence in her sculpting.

Back in New York, she earned a Master of Fine Arts degree from Columbia University. By now she was building a body of artistic work of her own, and she was becoming known for both her sculptures—human figures made from stone or wood but also at times brass, bronze, alabaster, or limestone—and for her teaching. Her sculptures of great Black Americans, such as Mary McLeod Bethune, Duke Ellington, and Booker T. Washington, graced public places. She continued teaching and, in 1940, opened the first of several art schools bearing her name, this one in New York City.

At the end of 1941, America entered World War II. Selma joined the Navy, becoming one of the first Black women to enlist. She worked as a truck driver in the Brooklyn Navy Yard. She told her friends she believed it was important to step away from art sometimes to live in the real world. And yet it was while she was in the Navy that she was commissioned to make a bas-relief portrait of the current president, Franklin Delano Roosevelt, for the Recorder of Deeds Building in Washington, DC.

Selma did her research to create an image of Roosevelt. She wanted something in profile, but no image of Roosevelt in profile seemed to exist. Being ever resourceful, she decided to try something daring and contacted the White House. Would the president be willing to sit for some sketches? She was able to speak to him personally on the phone. She told him she had a Ford car and could drive to him—would he see her? He agreed to sit for her for a brief time that day. So off to the White House Selma went. It all happened so fast that she didn't have her sketchbook with her, so she stopped at a butcher shop and obtained a roll of white meatpacking paper to sketch on.

That first sitting stretched to two hours, and two more sittings with Roosevelt were scheduled so that she could make sketches of him in profile. She reported that he was a friendly man but at first very wiggly. Like the good teacher she was, she mildly scolded the leader of the free world to sit still. And he did.

Roosevelt sat a second time for Selma, but he died unexpectedly before the third sitting could take place. Selma took what she had and created sketches of Roosevelt's image in profile, featuring a raised head and a prominently raised chin—not a pose people usually saw of this man.

When her sketches were finished, former first lady Eleanor Roosevelt came to Selma's home to view the work. Mrs. Roosevelt was known for many good things, including her good manners. But she felt compelled to admit she didn't like this image of her beloved late husband. It didn't look like how she saw him. His forehead was too high. And he looked too young.

Artist Selma took no offense. She explained that she wanted to show a great man looking to the future. "I didn't make it for today," she said. "I made it for tomorrow and tomorrow. Five hundred years from now, America and all the world will want to look at our president, not as he was for the few months before he died, but as we saw him for the time he was with us—strong, so full of life."

After that comment, Mrs. Roosevelt endorsed the image. Selma began working on the bas-relief in bronze. The result—a bronze plaque measuring 42 × 30 inches—was unveiled in the Recorder of Deeds Building on September 24, 1945, and it can be seen there still.

In 1946, an event shook up Selma's world. The United States Mint issued a new dime. It had a profile image of Roosevelt on it, signed with the initials J. S., standing for John Sinnock, an engraver for the Mint. It became clear to Selma and to others—including the Smithsonian Art Museum and the late president's own son—that Sinnock had used her profile of Roosevelt, making only a few changes and calling it his.

But Sinnock was adamant that he had not copied her work. It is true that Sinnock's image and Selma Burke's images are not identical. The foreheads are different, for example, because Sinnock took Mrs. Roosevelt's suggestion that the forehead was too high and "fixed" it. But despite these minor alterations, it was clear to experts and those in Roosevelt's circle that this was the work of Selma Burke.

When Selma recognized her work, she requested an investigation so that she could receive rightful credit for it. Instead, she found herself under investigation by the FBI. It was not unusual for Black Americans with a certain amount of fame to live with FBI intimidation to some degree, though nothing came of that investigation.

Nothing came of Selma's request for an investigation, either. Even though many organizations, artists, and numismatists (people who study coins) credited the dime's image to Selma Burke, the official decision of the US Mint was to call her work only a partial inspiration for what appeared on the dime. They continued to credit Sinnock. Of course, Selma was not happy with that decision, but she moved on with her life and her work.

In 1949, Selma fell in love and married an architect named Herman Kobbe. They moved to Pennsylvania. Her first husband had only lived a year into their marriage, and, sadly, her second husband lived only six years into their marriage. He died in 1955, and Selma continued to live in Pennsylvania. She became very active there in helping inner-city youth have opportunities in art.

It was always clear to Selma that she had been blessed to have a supportive family who understood her artistic soul and encouraged her talents—especially for the times and circumstances of her childhood. While there was always an extra struggle for Black people to live well, be educated, and follow their individual dreams, Selma was privileged to grow up celebrating the fact that she was a unique child of God. She wanted other children—in particular, Black children—to have that same kind of celebration in their lives. She knew that education and art would contribute to that.

Selma had been able to see the world, but most Black children did not fare as well throughout the twentieth century. When she learned one day that in her hometown of Mooresville Black children were still not allowed to use the public library, she found a creative way to change things. She offered to sculpt a bust of a local doctor and donate it to the town—on the condition that the ban at the library be lifted. Selma Burke was a nationally admired artist by then, and her hometown accepted her offer. Black children began using the public library.

She sculpted well into her old age, and her work can be seen in public places throughout the country to this day. She referred to herself as "a people's sculptor," in that she wanted her work to be easy to understand for people without formal training in art. The internet is full of images of her wonderful work. Even at age eighty, she was making beautiful sculptures. She created a nine-foot bronze statue of Martin Luther King Jr. that stands in Marshall Park in Charlotte, North Carolina.

After those many years of controversy, Selma was finally recognized as the artist of Roosevelt's image on the dime, and fortunately she lived to see it. The Bush administration righted that wrong in 1990. Five years later, this extraordinary teacher and one of the twentieth century's most notable sculptors died of cancer at age ninety-four in the town that had been her home for more than forty years: New Hope, Pennsylvania. Her ashes were scattered over the nearby Delaware River.

Today, each time we handle an American dime, we can ponder and enjoy Selma's vision of a beloved American leader as he looks confidently into the future.

LET'S REVIEW

1. What was the first thing Selma sculpted, and what happened to it?

2. Why didn't Selma's mother want her to focus her career solely on art? What did Selma do to placate her mother?

3. Why wasn't Eleanor Roosevelt pleased with the image of her husband as Selma portrayed him? What was Selma's response?

LET'S DO MORE

Can you create a visual profile of someone? Use pencil, chalk, paint, magic markers, needlework, or whatever suits you, and try creating a profile of a person or animal in your life or from history.

CHARLESZETTA "MOTHER" WADDLES

(1912–2001)

Mission Founder

"No one is too poor to help those who are less fortunate."

Baby, show me what you've done," Momma called from the next room to her twelve-year-old daughter.

The girl turned off the burner on the gas stove. She took two potholders and hefted the large iron skillet full of browning hamburger meat. She felt lucky that she'd found a half pound of it on sale at the butcher shop this afternoon. It would make tonight's meal so much better.

She carried the skillet into the next room and up to Momma's bed. "See?" she said. "I watched the flame like you said."

Momma looked at the meat and inhaled a little. "Very good, child. Now stir in the onion. And a teaspoon of pepper too. Then I'll tell you how to make tomato sauce. You got the water ready for the noodles?"

The girl nodded. Just last week, she had been in eighth grade at school, making excellent grades. She was a very intelligent student who loved to read and to write poetry. But things were hard at home, and she realized on her own that she would need to drop out of school because of it. She didn't spend time wishing it were otherwise—she knew she was needed. She was the oldest in the family, and Daddy had recently died. Momma had been bedbound for a long time. Now the doctor said Momma was dying too.

When the child told her mother that she would be taking care of things now, all Momma could do was nod. Already this oldest child was doing all the cleaning, washing, and ironing, and now she was learning to cook. Shortly after Daddy died, Momma had given birth to a baby girl. Big Sister cared for the baby part of the time too.

The child had gained her adult height and looked older than she was, so she had no trouble finding a job as a housemaid. Now Momma was teaching her how to cook supper for the household after work. In those days, when food was not available already prepared, getting a meal together wasn't as easy as it looked. But tonight's spaghetti with meat sauce was going to be a success. Every step of the way, Momma called her to bring the pot or skillet to the bed to be checked. And it looked like maybe cooking came naturally to the girl.

She took the pan back to the stove and lit a match to fire up the burner again. Then she turned to the peeled onion to start chopping. After showing Momma her progress two more times, the girl had supper ready.

The front door opened, and she watched her younger sister come in from school. She saw her breathe in the warm, heavy fragrance of meat and starch, tomatoes and onions, then smile from ear to ear.

She smiled back. "Supper's ready," she said.

The child had found her calling. She already knew that life was a strange thing, though faith could get you through. But she also knew that a simple thing like a hot meal could make people feel stronger. Big Sister realized she could do this every day by ensuring her sister and mother had a hot meal together. And Momma was so glad. "I wish I had a heart like yours," Momma told her.

Little did the child know that she would be cooking to feed people in need for the rest of her very productive life—and leading others to do the same. She would feed people even when she had almost nothing herself, cooking on her "Iron Horse," the name she gave her stove. She

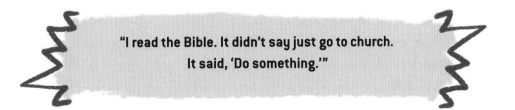

"I read the Bible. It didn't say just go to church. It said, 'Do something.'"

would believe deep in her heart that this was what God wanted her to do—not only to feed the hungry but to clothe the poor and house the homeless. In the process, she would offer dignity to those who suffered.

She would be called a "one-woman war on poverty" by her peers. Her creative, fearless, and loving ways of meeting her community's physical and spiritual needs were going to last throughout her lifetime and long beyond.

———

Charleszetta Lena Campbell was born in 1912 in St. Louis, Missouri. Her parents were Henry Campbell and Ella Brown Campbell. They had seven children, but only three of them survived beyond age two—Charleszetta and her two younger sisters.

For many years, her father was a successful barber in St. Louis, and the Campbell family lived well. But one day he unknowingly cut the hair of a customer who had impetigo, a highly contagious skin disease. Barbershops had ways of keeping things sanitary, but for some reason, this time the disease spread to several other clients. These were the days before antibiotics, and a skin disease could disfigure a person and take precious time to heal.

Some of those clients who caught impetigo attended the same church as the Campbell family, and those clients turned on Henry. So did the rest of the church. Henry Campbell lost his livelihood virtually overnight. He never found meaningful work again. It broke his spirit, and being shunned by his church friends broke his heart. He took to aimlessly wandering around St. Louis until he died, leaving two young children and a pregnant wife behind with no source of income.

Charleszetta remembered that chain of events the rest of her life—how one mistake at the barbershop caused her happy home to fall apart. Her father lost his job and his reputation in a public, shaming way. The family had to move to a cheaper house. Then her father died, and none of his church friends even attended his funeral. Her widowed mother gave birth to a new baby, then was diagnosed with a serious illness and told she was dying. Charleszetta stepped up to take over at home by dropping out of the eighth grade and going to work as a maid. When that wasn't enough money to support the household, she took on another job in a factory sorting rags.

Since her mother was confined to her bed, Charleszetta also took over much of the parenting role for her sisters. Besides holding down outside jobs, she did all the housework and laundry for their home. Charleszetta never had much time to be a child herself. She grew up quickly.

At age fourteen, Charleszetta married and within a year gave birth to her first child. A few years after that, her husband died. She still helped with her mother and younger sisters. Happily, Momma did not die for many years and even remarried. Charleszetta also remarried and had several more children. Then she and her husband moved to Detroit. In total, Charleszetta would have ten children.

Detroit was a dynamic town at the time. The auto industry offered lots of opportunity and made the town hop in every way. Charleszetta raised her children and worked. Then her husband abandoned the family. She spent many years as a single mother of ten children, and times were very difficult. But she always had her faith.

Charleszetta put great stock in reading the Bible. She believed in concentrating on the New Testament and its "red words," which were the words spoken by Christ, printed in red in some Bibles. She was particularly influenced by Matthew 25:31–46, where Christ instructs his believers to feed the hungry, clothe them, and offer them shelter.

This is where Christ says that helping "the least of these" honors him. Charleszetta took that to heart.

During this time of financial difficulty, she started a prayer group with other women like herself—all of them were poor and had many children. They took their eyes off their own problems and looked for how they could help others. These women had almost nothing to offer in a material way, but they found ways to be helpful nonetheless. They came to believe that nobody was too poor to help someone else. If someone needed a bed, they'd find a bed someone else didn't need. If someone needed clothes for a job, they'd find nice hand-me-downs from other people or from thrift stores.

One day, one of the women in the group had a new problem. Her husband had died suddenly and left her and her children without any means of financial support. Now the family was behind on their house payment. The woman could lose her home, and she and her children would be on the street.

Charleszetta didn't have money to give her friend—none of the women did—but she did have a creative mind and a persuasive personality. She strategized to have all the people she could find donate food to the woman's house—enough to feed her and her children for one month, so that whatever she would have had to pay in groceries could now be used to pay her house payment. Such support helped the woman get back on her feet.

Charleszetta continued to help others. Always a strong Christian, she became an ordained minister in the Pentecostal church. She also started a restaurant for the needy. The Helping Hand Restaurant served home-cooked meals—Charleszetta cooked them herself on her Iron Horse—for only thirty-five cents. If a customer couldn't afford it, they could pay whatever they could or eat free. Unlike the more typical soup kitchen lines for the poor that had sprung up in cities, Helping Hand Restaurant had tables with tablecloths and waitresses serving the customers. In these ways, people were able to maintain their dignity.

In 1956, Charleszetta talked a man into renting her a storefront space for free. That is where she founded what she named Detroit's Perpetual Mission for Saving Souls for All Nations. The Mission fed hungry people and offered clothing and furniture for the needy. As time went on, the Perpetual Mission would also offer job training, help with low-cost housing, medical services, and legal services. They also had a jail and prison mission.

Charleszetta believed in helping people in their spiritual walk too, so the Mission offered classes and studies to grow in one's faith. She was also committed to helping people not stay mired in a life of poverty but rather improve their situation. Eventually, the city of Detroit's social services agencies even sent people in need to the Perpetual Mission.

At times a person would have a more personal need—for example, parents needed to buy school pictures or athletic uniforms for their kids. The Mission figured out how to help. Sometimes moms couldn't afford to buy a dress for their daughters for the school prom. But Charleszetta and her people made sure those girls had a prom dress.

One day in 1957, Charleszetta cooked up some pots of barbecue in the front yard of her church to sell. She was known for these very popular fundraisers. It seemed like whenever soul food was served at the church, all of Detroit showed up. That day, a Ford worker named Payton Waddles came for some home-cooked barbecue. A perfect gentleman, he helped the church ladies throughout the day and in the process got to know Charleszetta. He stuck around. They married later that year.

Payton was supportive of Charleszetta and the Mission from day one. He became so beloved that everyone called him "Daddy," much like by now they were calling Charleszetta "Mother."

The year 1967 was a time of unrest throughout America. In Detroit, a riot broke out in the summer and lasted for five days, during which forty-three people were killed, thousands were arrested, and around five thousand people lost their homes to fire and damage. It was a frightening time. The city went on lockdown and all businesses were closed because of looting. But Mother Waddles, as she was now known, hit the streets anyway to deliver food, clothes, and other essentials to people.

Detroiters never forgot this. The name Mother Waddles became known and highly respected. She continued to feed and serve. Her next project was a cookbook, *The Mother Waddles Soul Food Cookbook*. It contained her favorite meals she served to family, friends, and communities, and she sold the book to raise funds for the needy.

Mother Waddles and her impressive work were featured in dozens of major magazines, including *Newsweek*, *Ebony*, and *Reader's Digest*. These periodicals loved interviewing this ordinary yet extraordinary woman. "We're trying to show what the church could mean to the world if it lived by what it preached," Charleszetta told *Newsweek*. "I read the Bible. It didn't say just go to church. It said, 'Do something.'" To *Reader's Digest*, she said, "We give a person the things he needs, when he needs them. We take care of him whether he's an alcoholic or a junkie, Black or white, employed or unemployed. We don't turn anyone away."

In her later years, Mother Waddles won many awards for her service and was inducted into the Michigan Hall of Fame. She died in 2001 at the age of eighty-eight. All of Detroit grieved. Although neither the restaurant nor the church buildings stand today, her work goes on in her name. Billboards all over Detroit remind the needy that help is just a step away at Mother Waddles Perpetual Mission. Her compassion continues.

It was Charleszetta herself who perhaps best summed up what she did with her life in her own rhyme:

> Remember . . . creating a meal is a poor woman's thing,
> All she needs is imagination and a gospel song to sing.

LET'S REVIEW

1. How did Charleszetta's family go from respected and prosperous to shunned and poor?
2. Why did Charleszetta move to Detroit?
3. What major event in Detroit made its citizens especially respect Charleszetta?

LET'S DO MORE

Is there something you hope to do to make the world better? Try your hand at poetry like Mother Waddles did, and tell about it. Write a poem of any length or a song about what you could do to make the world a better place.

KATHERINE GOBLE JOHNSON

(1918–2020)

NASA Analyst

"Like what you do, and then you will do your best."

She was a smart and chatty little girl. She had constant questions about everything as soon as she could speak—questions asked not because she craved attention but because she was so curious. The child badgered her older siblings while they did their homework— not because she wanted to annoy them but because she truly wanted to learn what they were learning. When her mother, a teacher, grew weary of answering her youngest child's nonstop questions, she taught the preschooler how to read and how to understand numbers.

The little girl happily learned to read right away. Her parents were pleased by this, but it was when they observed her arithmetic skills that they knew she was really an extraordinary child. She was a prodigy— someone with exceptional talent or knowledge in an area, with abilities well beyond their age. In her case, she was a whiz at mathematics. She was fascinated by numbers and their challenges. She counted everything— how many steps from home to church, how many dishes and pieces of silverware she washed and dried after supper. Anything that could be counted, she counted. She even tried to count the stars in the sky.

She started school at age four, and she relished every moment of learning. She was a Black child attending school in the segregated South, so books and supplies were shabby, used hand-me-downs from white schools. Fortunately, the teachers themselves were dedicated and creative, and the child soaked up everything they could teach her in any subject. She easily advanced, even skipping grades, until she completed elementary school at age ten.

In those days, Black children in the South seldom attended school beyond the eighth grade, but this brilliant little girl got to move on to high school. There she had more excellent teachers, including one who challenged her with, "What do you know today that you didn't know yesterday?" The child managed to think of something every day. "You have to be better today than you were yesterday," the teacher encouraged. It was a strong way to move forward in life.

In the meantime, her parents taught her how to get along in the world. They taught her to see the best in people and in situations and to work hard for her goals. Her father's life philosophy was, "You're as good as anybody else, but no better." That idea instilled in his daughter a confidence that would serve her well for her entire life.

By the time the child graduated from high school—at only age fourteen—her teachers and family members knew she was going places. But nobody could have dreamed how far—or that someday her brilliance would literally help blast off the first American astronauts straight into outer space . . . and onto the moon.

Until then, she kept counting the stars.

———

She was born Creola Katherine Coleman in White Sulphur Springs, West Virginia, in 1918, and everyone called her by her middle name. She grew up as a proud West Virginian. As a result of the Civil War, West Virginia had formed out of a part of the state of Virginia and declared its independence from the Confederacy. That legacy meant that when

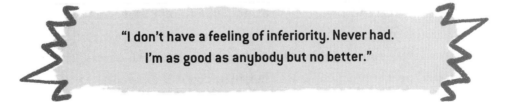

"I don't have a feeling of inferiority. Never had. I'm as good as anybody but no better."

Katherine was growing up, the heavy hand of racism was a little bit lighter. But it was never gone. It was always there.

Katherine was the youngest of four children raised by Joylette Roberta and Joshua McKinley Coleman. These smart and hardworking parents were respected in the community, were active in church, and believed strongly in the power of education. So, when the older children were finishing the eighth grade and there was no high school nearby for Black students to attend, their parents devised a plan. Mother and children moved about 130 miles away to spend the school year in Institute, West Virginia, a town that had a high school for Black students. Father stayed behind to work several jobs and support both households. It wasn't easy by any means, but it worked. All the children received their upper education at a good school, and Katherine felt tremendous gratitude to her parents for such sacrifices.

When fourteen-year-old Katherine graduated from high school, she went on to West Virginia State College. There she took every possible math class under excellent professors. She also joined Alpha Kappa Alpha, and these sorority sisters became lifelong friends.

During these years, Katherine was taught by one of her most influential professors, Dr. W. W. Schieffelin Claytor, the third African American to receive a PhD in mathematics. He was so impressed with Katherine's math abilities that, after he taught her all he could from the existing school curriculum, he developed a new advanced class for Katherine alone. He was the person who suggested she could be an excellent research mathematician.

A research mathematician was not something Katherine had ever heard of, but it sounded like a good career for her. Where could she get a job like that? She would not know for quite some time. In the meantime, her professor taught her all he could and encouraged her to build a personal library of math books to take with her on any future jobs in mathematics. She did as he suggested.

Katherine graduated from West Virginia State *summa cum laude* (meaning "with highest distinction") at age eighteen. She had majored in mathematics and music, and she became a teacher of both. A couple years into her teaching career, she met her future husband, Jimmie Goble, when the two of them were involved in a theatrical production. Soon they married and built a happy family with three daughters.

In 1953, Katherine managed to find work in the field she most desired to be in. She left teaching to be employed by the National Advisory Committee for Aeronautics (NACA) in Langley, Virginia. For a Black woman in America to land such a job was rare, and she would work there for the next three decades.

Her first job was as a computer. The word *computer* in those days did not mean what it means today—a highly sophisticated machine. It used to refer to the actual person who computed numbers—by hand. There were pools of women at NACA computing necessary information, and Katherine joined them. She referred to her coworkers and herself as "computers who wore skirts."

These were the days of keeping Black people and white people separated in public places in most areas in the South, sometimes by law and sometimes by unwritten policy. This included workplaces. So the Black computers performing high math tasks were in a different building than the white computers. The workers had to use different lunchrooms, restrooms, and water fountains based on their race. Whites were separated from Blacks in every way. That's how it was then.

Eventually Katherine packed up her collection of math books and moved out of the computer pool. Because of her math genius—and against all odds for a Black woman—she was moved to the Flight

Research Division. Now she worked with white male engineers all day. She and her team tested flights in the air, researching how to prevent crashes. They also analyzed turbulence, a very important factor in air safety. This was hands-on work using her excellent brainpower to save lives. Katherine always loved it when math impacted the real world.

Alongside the racial segregation in the workplace, women in general were treated as second-class citizens at NACA in those days, much like they were in many workplaces. Katherine ran head-on into this. Nobody suggested she wasn't smart; they knew she was extremely smart. But this large agency and its leadership consisted of only men—specifically white men. They hadn't dealt with women in their field of work and didn't care to start.

Katherine asserted herself more than once to do what she knew she was good at doing. Fortunately, she had an energetic, dynamic, and charming personality. Because of her positive training from her parents, she was a person who let pettiness roll off her back, and she was never afraid to ask questions. When she needed to be part of frequent strategy meetings that impacted her work—meetings she was not invited to—she spoke up. The men in the meeting explained that women were simply not allowed. What they really said was that "girls" were not allowed. They respected Katherine's intelligence, but she could not come to the meeting because she was female.

Katherine knew her colleagues were logical men, so she asked if the attendance of a woman was actually against the law. There was only a surprised silence in the room. Katherine again stated the reasons she should be included in the meetings, and from then on began attending the strategy meetings she knew she should attend. The only woman. The only Black person.

Usually Katherine was able to move on and stay positive, regardless of the indignity of injustice. But the one time she was unable to let such things roll off her back was the day the Gobles were visiting the home of a white coworker. As the children played in the yard, one of the Goble girls was injured, with a deep cut to her head.

Everyone hurried to the nearest hospital emergency room. But the workers there refused to treat the child. Why? Because they did not treat Black people—not even a child with a head injury. Katherine's white friend used all his influence to try to get them to make an exception for this injured child. They would not.

Katherine was horrified. They were unable to find treatment for her child until the next day. *What if the injury had been worse?* Katherine thought. That kind of frightening injustice always hovered around, and no amount of positive spirit could ignore it. It was reality.

In 1957, the National Advisory Committee for Aeronautics changed its name to the National Aeronautics and Space Administration, known as NASA even today. NASA expanded beyond designing aircraft to designing spaceships. There was a competition going on at the time between America and another world power, the Soviet Union, as to who would succeed first and foremost in space. The Soviets were ahead; they had sent a satellite known as Sputnik into space.

This was exciting to the entire world. But American leaders did not like being behind in this "space race." There was also fear that conquering space could be a security issue for nations on earth. NASA got busy planning space flights, including a mission to go to the moon one day.

Now working as an aerospace technologist, Katherine truly made her mark in these early days of the space race. The laboratory team worked day and night to plan a flight for astronaut John Glenn—to send him into space and bring him back home safely. It had never been done by the Americans before.

Of course, Katherine knew mathematics would do the work. She told her superior, "Tell me where you want his spaceship to land, and I'll tell you where to launch it from." Then she plotted it out mathematically. Katherine impressed both her boss and John Glenn with her confidence and exact calculations.

When the time came for John Glenn to make final preparations for his mission, he told NASA he wanted Katherine specifically to calculate by hand the numbers NASA's engineers had calculated for his flight trajectory. He felt that if brilliant Katherine's math backed up the plan, he would be safe. (This is beautifully dramatized in the movie *Hidden Figures*.)

Katherine confirmed the numbers. The mission launched successfully on February 20, 1962. John Glenn flew into space and circled the earth. It all happened safely, thanks to NASA and to Katherine.

During Katherine's time at Langley, tragedy hit her home when they learned her husband, Jimmie, had untreatable brain cancer. After only sixteen years of marriage, Jimmie died, leaving Katherine with three young daughters. Family, church, and the Langley friends were helpful in keeping the Goble family going emotionally.

Katherine threw herself into her work and into keeping her girls secure. During these years, the Civil Rights Movement grew in strength. Dr. Martin Luther King Jr. rose to prominence, then was horribly gunned down. Many other lives were lost in the racial issues of those days, and times were grim. But change began to come. Laws started to change. Institutions were integrated, even in the South. Katherine was hopeful for her children, that the way forward might be safer and more respectful for them. Maybe they would never have to fret over their own injured child because a hospital refused to treat Black people.

A few years after Jimmie died, Katherine met her next husband in the choir at the church she'd been attending for years. His name was James, too—they called him Jim. He and Katherine were married, and happily so, for the next sixty years until his death.

At NASA, Katherine continued working on missions that would become historically famous. She was involved in configuring the moon landing in 1969. She watched the event itself on television along with the rest of the world. She shared that moment with her sorority sisters at a convention. While everyone cheered at the landing, Katherine knew she would feel much better once the crew was safely back on earth. Fortunately, the mission was successful all the way.

Another famous mission she worked on was Apollo 13 in 1970, immortalized by a movie of the same name. When the ship became disabled in space with three astronauts on board, Katherine was one of the main forces on the ground working to bring it home safely. She also worked on many shuttles at NASA until her retirement after thirty-three years of service.

Katherine lived a very long life. In her retirement, she spoke to groups and to children about her experiences at NASA and about STEM—science, technology, engineering, and mathematics. She especially wanted Black children to reach for the stars, so to speak, as she did. She wanted them to know they could do so much in this world. She encouraged them to consider pursuing a career in STEM for their own futures.

In her later years, Katherine received many awards, and a full list can be found online. Buildings were named after her. In 2015, Katherine was awarded the Presidential Medal of Freedom by President Barack Obama, the first Black American president. Noting that she was one of the first Black scientists to work at NASA, he said, "Katherine G. Johnson refused to be limited by society's expectations of her gender and race while expanding the boundaries of humanity's reach." After he placed a medallion around her neck, he kissed her cheek. For quite some time, women asked Katherine how it felt to be kissed by President Obama. Katherine would beam and comment, "All I can say is it was thrilling."

In 2016, the book *Hidden Figures* by Margot Shetterly was published. It profiled several Black women from NASA's early days in the space race, including Katherine. Later that year, a Hollywood movie was released based on the book and covered the lives of Katherine (played by Taraji P. Henson) and two other real-life NASA colleagues, Dorothy Vaughn and Mary Jackson.

Katherine thought the movie was very good and was pleased with Henson's performance. Although by now Katherine was elderly and not in strong health, the Academy invited her to its awards ceremony. She agreed to be flown to Los Angeles from Virginia with her daughters to be present when the movie was honored with nominations. This was an exciting event for her, and she dressed elegantly for it.

That evening, she was brought onstage and was stunned to receive a standing ovation. Actress Taraji P. Henson approached Katherine and her daughters and asked them, "Did I do all right?" There were many tears all around. Later the actress would report that playing Katherine was her favorite acting role, because "It's had the most amazing, positive impact on our community and girls in general."

But maybe the most fun honor was when Mattel created the Katherine Goble Johnson Barbie doll, complete with Katherine's signature cat glasses. The doll even wore an ID badge from NASA.

Katherine lived to enjoy six grandchildren and eleven great-grandchildren—all of whom she encouraged to pursue careers in STEM. She died in 2020 at age 101, only one year after her beloved husband, Jim.

Think about the world changes this amazing woman saw during her century on the planet—the Great Depression, two World Wars and many other wars, two pandemics, so many medical and scientific accomplishments, the space race. As Katherine so well expressed, "You have to expect progress to be made."

She could well have added, "And you have to help it happen."

The remarkable Katherine Goble Johnson showed us how it's done.

LET'S REVIEW

1. How old was Katherine when she graduated from high school?
2. Who was the first astronaut to know Katherine's work? In what ways did it affect him?
3. The movie *Hidden Figures* showcased Katherine and two other NASA Black women. Who were they?

LET'S DO MORE

When Katherine's math professor had taught her everything in the curriculum, he created another class for her alone. Is there something you'd like to learn that isn't in your school studies? What is it? How can you find a way to learn it? Devise a plan and write it down—and see where it goes.

ALICE COACHMAN

(1923–2014)

Olympic Gold Medalist

"I've always believed I could do whatever I set my mind to do."

The teenage girl stepped outside her house on a sunny Georgia morning with butterflies in her stomach. Lean and long-legged, she was fifteen going on sixteen, and today she found herself in the most exciting situation. She learned that she was going to compete in track and field events—on a college team. She could hardly believe it.

It was 1939, a time when her world had very little interest in the athletic ability of one Black female teenager. In those days, athletic opportunities were hard to come by for any female, much less a Black girl still in high school. But the young woman's talent and work ethic were clear to see. She also had determination. Once this teenager got a goal in her head, that goal would be met.

Her parents understood this track team was a rare opportunity for their daughter. They just wished it were a different opportunity. Their ideas about what girls should and shouldn't do were traditional and in keeping with the times, so they had trouble seeing their daughter as an athlete. They would rather all of their girls focus on learning the housewife skills they would need when they married and had children. Nevertheless, they stood by their daughter when she was offered a position on the college team at such an early age. They chose to put their concerns aside and trust the child they had raised.

There were no gyms available to this young athlete. She worked out at home, and that included running barefoot on the red Georgia clay roads. She built equipment in their backyard, using planks of wood and rope to practice high jumps. She developed her own idea on how to successfully hydrate when performing. She'd pick a lemon from one of the trees that grew around her, stab a hole in its skin, and suck out its juice. It was just enough liquid to hydrate her while running and jumping and yet keep her light on her feet. She believed water slowed her down. But really, nothing would slow this girl down.

She stretched toward the sun climbing in the sky. Now she pulled a lemon out of her pocket, squeezed out its juice, and then tossed the rind into a field. She wiggled her long bare toes on top of the hard Georgia clay and off she went on her daily run—and eventually to her first gold medal and an amazing life.

———

Alice Coachman was born in 1923 to Fred and Evelyn Coachman in Albany, Georgia. She was the fifth of ten children. She was raised by good, hardworking people. But even hardworking people could be poor, and the Coachman family was indeed poor.

Alice grew to be an excellent athlete. But as an athlete, she had two things working against her. She was a girl at a time when being female did not easily allow one to be an athlete. And she was Black when there was little equality in America for Blacks in any regard, particularly in the Deep South. Athletic opportunities were hard to come by.

At the same time, Alice also had two things working *for* her. She had an excellent fifth grade teacher, Cora Bailey, who encouraged Alice's talents in every area. Alice also had a particularly attentive, loving aunt named Corrie Spry. These two women were truly a double blessing, since Alice was one of many children in her home and could not always

"You're never more of an individual than when you're a happy team player."

receive much individual attention from her parents. They were both working hard to feed the family. Miss Bailey and Aunt Corrie each took a special interest in Alice's future and helped her negotiate a system that could work against Black girl athletes.

Young Alice was a lean 5 feet, 5½ inches tall. She excelled in all sports, especially basketball and track and field events, though the high jump would become her specialty. But when her mother watched her daughter in track and field events, Momma felt uncomfortable about it. It seemed odd to her, a girl running and jumping.

So Momma made certain her daughter had an attribute she could carry with her through life: modesty. She reminded Alice, "You're no better than anyone else. The people you pass on the ladder will be the same people you'll be with when the ladder comes down." Alice would always take that to heart and often quote her mother on this. She knew she was good enough to compete and win, but she would never be puffed up with pride.

Dad Fred especially did not like the idea that his daughter played sports. It didn't seem natural to him. He wanted Alice to act like his perception of femininity. He truly believed women were not meant to run, and he wasn't alone in thinking this way in 1939. There were little to no organized sports teams for young females. More traditional people believed females were literally not meant to move their bodies in the extreme ways required by sports. Consequently, most of the time growing up, Alice had played sports only with boys.

In his house, Dad wanted to see his idea of ladylike, stay-at-home daughters. But though he may have wanted Alice indoors sewing and cooking, the reality was that, while attending high school, she picked cotton and other crops to supplement the family income. It was understandably hard for parents to support ten children, so all the kids worked in the fields to help out. Alice showed herself to be a very capable young person who clearly could do far more than embroidery.

Alice's parents may not have wanted their girl to be athletic, but, to their credit, they did not stop their talented daughter from going after her dreams. And Alice's dreams were clear to her. One was to be an athlete. The other was to get out of poverty.

With all due respect to her hardworking family, young Alice did not want cotton fields in her future, and she did not want to be poor. She had reason to believe that sports could lift her out of poverty. So her parents stood back and let her fly, simply instilling good values in their child as they readied her to step out of the security of home.

At Madison High School, Alice joined the track team. That year, 1938, the Tuskegee Institute in Alabama noticed her and offered her a scholarship to Tuskegee Preparatory School. She was not yet sixteen. Imagine going from living in the country surrounded by a huge family to moving into a dormitory with strangers. It was a big change, but Alice learned how to deal with changes. The scholarship required her to work for the school while she trained and studied. Of course, this teenager already knew how to work. In exchange for her tuition, she cleaned the training facilities and mended uniforms.

Alice's athletic career kicked off quickly when she won a gold medal in the Amateur Athletic Union in 1939. This was a big step up at her young age, and Alice applied herself fully to her goals. She would go on to win a national championship award every year after that through 1948.

In her college years, Alice's athletic victories were well documented. But also documented was a disturbing rumor. The American press reported that while Alice was an amazing athlete, she was not much of a student. There was and is no indication that this was true; rather, it promoted a belief that Black athletes had "natural" ability when it came to physical accomplishments but little ability when it came to intellectual pursuits. The idea that a Black American could excel both physically and mentally was simply not accepted by many American whites. And whites ran the media.

This didn't stop Alice's dreams. Like the phenomenal high jumper she became, she seemed to soar above such pettiness.

World War II broke out while Alice was in her competition years, and the Olympics were canceled twice during the war. These were prime years for an athlete like Alice, and missing that international competition mattered. But Alice chose to focus on the competitions she could enter until finally, in 1948, the Olympics were back. Alice Coachman would now see the world.

On a rainy day in London, England, Alice competed in the high jump and became the first Black American female to bring home a gold medal. (One wonders where she got her lemons in foggy London!) She also set an Olympic record in field events. As she took her place on the podium to receive her medal, Alice heard the opening strains of "The Star-Spangled Banner." That's when her accomplishment truly sank in. The gold medal was presented to Alice by England's beloved and inspiring wartime king, George VI.

Upon her return to the States, Alice was invited to the White House to be congratulated by President Harry S. Truman, who expressed the pride of the nation at her wins. Her hometown of Albany, Georgia, held an "Alice Coachman Day" with a parade and a ceremony. But it was a town that was still very segregated. It's hard to believe today that at such an event, Blacks and whites could not sit next to each other in the auditorium where Alice was honored. The town's white mayor even refused to shake her hand.

But Alice took it in stride, as she was prone to do. Looking back on that event years later, she said, "We had segregation, but it wasn't any problem for me because I had won. That was up to them, whether they accepted it or not."

In 1946, Alice graduated with a degree in dressmaking from the Tuskegee Institute, then moved on to Albany State College in Georgia. She received her bachelor's degree there in 1949 in home economics with a minor in science. Her folks most likely sighed with relief at their daughter's choices to major in dressmaking and home economics.

Alice stopped competing in sports in 1949. She said she'd achieved her goals, and now she wanted to redirect her life—to teach, find a husband, and have a family. And she did all of that. She taught and coached track and field, married and became Alice Coachman Davis, and raised two children in Albany, Georgia.

Before she stepped away completely, however, Alice took on a major endorsement in the 1950s. Today we see athletes of all races endorsing products, but that was not the case in Alice's time. She became the first Black female athlete to be a spokesperson for an international product when, alongside the great Black Olympian Jessie Owens, she endorsed Coca-Cola. That visibility meant that millions of Black people could see and be inspired by the image of Americans who looked like them.

For the rest of her days, however, Alice Coachman remained out of public view. Having learned from her mother to be modest, Alice kept her accomplishments to herself until her last few years. Only then did she share the history of her athletic victories with her son and daughter.

Alice Coachman died in her hometown of Albany, Georgia, at the age of ninety. Ultimately, her legacy is one of overcoming and excelling. Nothing stood in the way of this bright and talented woman. She was not simply the holder of a list of firsts. Alice's successes also flung open the doors for future female Black American athletes, such as track and field legends Wilma Rudolph, Florence Griffith Joyner, Jackie Joyner-Kersee, and so many more. Alice took that legacy to heart, saying, "If I had gone to the Games and failed, there wouldn't be anyone to follow in my footsteps. It encouraged the rest of the women to work harder and fight harder."

Famous Black female track and field athletes today know who paved their way. She was the barefoot Georgia girl who consumed lemon juice to stay light on her feet—who soared over the jumps and straight into the imaginations and the dreams of other Black girl athletes, leaving behind her legacy.

LET'S REVIEW

1. Where did Alice work out as a young teenager?
2. Why were her parents hesitant about Alice's athleticism?
3. What product did Alice endorse? With whom?

LET'S DO MORE

List as many Black American women Olympians as you can think of. Start with track and field, then go on from there. Pick one to research. Imagine she's speaking with Alice Coachman. What are they saying to each other?

CICELY TYSON

(1924–2021)

Actress

"I have learned not to allow rejection to move me."

Her father adored her from the moment she was born. He doted on this frail and tiny infant who grew to be shy, ever-watchful, and nearly silent. Her thumb was in her mouth most of her first twelve years, resulting in a slight overbite of her front teeth she carried for the rest of her life.

One Sunday, Daddy wanted to take his favorite child to his mother's Baptist church. He asked her if she might want to sing for the congregation. The child had just finished a starring role in her own Episcopal church's Sunday school Christmas production as Mary, the mother of Jesus, and she had found she enjoyed that. Performing for a crowd of people from the stage felt easier to her than talking to people one at a time. She nodded to her father. Her mother dressed her in a velvet dress she had sewn for her, lace-trimmed socks, and shiny Mary Jane shoes. Off the child went, her tiny hand tucked into Daddy's large one.

At the Baptist church, Daddy led her to the stage area where the minister introduced the tiny seven-year-old to the congregation. *What now?* Suddenly, the usually timid little girl felt something new inside herself—a purpose. A reason for being there in front of all these people. It was a powerful feeling that surged through her. She took her thumb out of her mouth and looked around at the congregation. Then she began to sing at the top of her lungs.

Half singing, half yelling, she belted out a popular church song of the day, a lively one in which the singer starts each verse by singing, "How do you do?" to everyone in church. The organist found the key and started pounding away on the keyboard to accompany the child. The congregation went wild.

As the little girl continued into the next verse, four of the church's elders picked her up and sat her down on a chair. Then each grabbed a chair leg and swiftly hoisted the featherweight girl into the air. They marched her down the church aisle while the excited congregation hollered back responses to the child's "How do you do?" Her skinny legs dangled from the chair as she sang louder and higher.

When it was all over and the people in the church called out their appreciation, a new confidence filled the child. Even at the tender age of seven, she realized she was destined to use the talents she had been given—talents that could stir a crowd—from now on.

She was never shy again.

———

She was born Cicely Louise Tyson in New York City's Harlem in 1924. Her parents, Fredericka Huggins Tyson and William Augustine Tyson, were immigrants from Nevis, an island in the West Indies. They moved to New York City as young adults and married. Each worked more than one job at a time to support their family as it grew.

Cicely, usually called Sis, was the middleborn of three children and her father's clear favorite. She was not only exceptionally tiny at birth but also diagnosed with a heart murmur. The doctor told her parents she would not likely live past three months.

"Challenges make you discover things about yourself that you never really knew. They're what make the instrument stretch—what makes you go beyond the norm."

But the Tysons chose to believe otherwise. They prayed and asked their church to do the same. Their baby survived infancy. In her toddler years, her parents did their best to fatten their baby up with Mom's excellent cooking. They believed added weight would make her healthy. But she remained so lean that her father nicknamed her String Bean. Little Cicely was so nurtured and loved that she not only survived but thrived.

The Tyson family was deeply religious. They alternated between attending an Episcopal church and a Baptist church. Cicely and her siblings went to church every Sunday morning, Sunday night, and several weeknights for prayer meetings or choir practice.

Mom was an excellent seamstress who enjoyed sewing lovely dresses and jackets for her children to wear to church services. As she created these clothes or cooked the Sunday meal, she sang. Hymns were the music of the Tyson house, and everyone sang all the verses. Mom's favorite hymn was "Blessed Assurance," and little Cicely's favorite was "Just as I Am." Cicely grew to be a lifelong Christian who developed the practice of starting each morning with prayer and meditation on the lyrics to "Just as I Am."

But although there was love in the house, there was also strife. Too much strife. Both parents worked two or three jobs to make ends meet. The stresses of life made them fight so much at home that, when Cicely was eleven, her parents decided to separate. This was a tremendous heartbreak for Cicely. Fortunately, both parents stayed involved with their children, their churches, and even each other for the rest of their lives. They just didn't live together.

There was something else that was disturbing to young Cicely as a Black child. She grew up around a large extended family whose skin tones covered a spectrum from light to dark. Cicely was loved and held up as beautiful by her family, as were all the females. But outside of home, she discovered *colorism*—where Black people are judged by the varying shades of their skin.

Cicely's skin was a dark chestnut brown, and her hair was black with tight curls. After watching Black women in her world try to conform to the standards of beauty for white people, Cicely came to believe early on that she was not beautiful. She could have no idea how her sense of beauty would spin completely around once she became a grown woman.

Cicely grew up very close to each of her parents. Of course, she'd always had a close bond with Daddy, from the time he first held her. Even as a baby, she was put on his knee while he played guitar and sang to her. Her mother's favorite was Cicely's brother. Nevertheless, Cicely and Mom loved each other very deeply. They also annoyed each other, as strong relatives can. Mom's standards for respectability were very high, and although Cicely was a good church girl, she often had to deal with her mother's disapproval.

For one thing, Cicely married young, and her mother disapproved of this. She'd expected Cicely to go to college and then marry the "right" husband. But things didn't work out that way. Cicely married her high school boyfriend, who abandoned her after she had their daughter. Cicely would raise her child alone, though with some help from Mom. This daughter was the only child Cicely would have. It's not clear what she named her daughter, but to protect the child's privacy once Cicely started to gain fame, Cicely chose to refer to her simply as "Joan."

Cicely had a strong work ethic she learned from her hardworking parents, so she worked two or three jobs just as her parents had. One of her many jobs in her early twenties was working as a typist in Manhattan. She could type an impressive one hundred words per minute on a manual typewriter.

As she walked to work one day, a stranger asked her if she was a model. This shocked Cicely because she assumed she did not have the looks for such a job. Why would he think she was a model? But the stranger insisted she should model, and he gave her the name of a modeling agency to check out before they went about their ways.

Cicely was intrigued. Maybe she could earn more money modeling than typing, and she did have a child to support. She interviewed at the agency and was promptly hired, even though she was forthright about her lack of experience. It turned out there was a new appreciation for her more natural beauty and elegance. Being tall was not yet a requirement for modeling. Before long she was doing cover shots for *Ebony* and *Jet*, two major magazines for the Black readership. She made good wages modeling, though she kept her other jobs. Her concern was always how to support her child by herself.

At the modeling agency one day, she was approached by someone scouting for an actress. Cicely let the person know she had no acting experience. But the scout saw strong possibility in Cicely's appearance, movements, and style. Already the camera liked Cicely. It would be the same on the big screen. Her quiet beauty, large and expressive eyes, and compelling voice charmed viewers, even though the first movies she was in were not very successful. Nevertheless, she was making screen connections while she still modeled.

Unfortunately, Cicely's mother greatly disapproved of movies. This was for religious reasons. The church the family belonged to believed movie theaters were sinful places. Once Mom learned of Cicely's work on the big screen, she didn't speak to her for a year. In hindsight, Cicely would acknowledge that her mother simply acted the way she thought she was supposed to act by disapproving of movies so strongly.

But Cicely was an adult now, one who had developed a firm sense of her own purpose. Cicely's belief in God was strong, and she believed without a doubt that God wanted her to act—that he made her the way she was and was opening the avenues for her. Dare she not do what she was put here to do?

Even though Cicely and her mother did not communicate for so long, there were no lasting hard feelings. Cicely deeply respected her mother. And Mom eventually changed her mind about Cicely's chosen profession. It was seeing Cicely perform on the live stage that changed everything. On opening night of her first play, Cicely could hear her mother in the audience making amazed comments all through the performance. Mom was proud of her daughter and couldn't keep quiet about it!

During the years in which Cicely built her career as an actress, before she was well known, she had to leave home for long periods to work on location. She left her daughter, Joan, for weeks at a time. Joan was safe and well cared for, but the relationship between mother and daughter suffered. Cicely realized years later that providing for her daughter by being away from home so much had taken over sharing daily life together. They both suffered from that distance, but they worked on their relationship when Joan was grown. Joan always was the blessing of Cicely's life.

Cicely's career turned to television when she costarred with the great actor George C. Scott in an excellent but short-lived CBS series called *East Side, West Side.* This drama was ahead of its time. Networks and their sponsors only played to white audiences then, as if they didn't realize—or care—that Black people were watching too. Seldom did Black people appear on television at all in those days, and when they did, they usually played servants, slaves, or criminals.

That was not so in *East Side, West Side*. The core cast was integrated, plus the plots were often about race, the characters were well written, and the guest stars numbered almost as many Blacks as whites. This was very rare for primetime television in those early days, and it was many years before another TV series offered as much. Although the series only lasted one season, it jump-started or advanced the careers of many Black American actors, including Cicely Tyson.

In this TV series, Cicely caused quite a stir by choosing to wear her hair short and natural. This was the Afro hairstyle, which was not yet in vogue, though it would become very popular as the sixties moved on. At first, though, it was considered radical for Black women to wear their hair as it grew naturally rather than try to imitate white hair styles that required chemical straightening and hot combs. These reactions came from both white people and some Black people.

Nevertheless, Black women were growing tired of a white standard of beauty. They found they liked the natural look and its easy care. The Afro in many lengths became extremely popular, thanks to people like Cicely Tyson.

It was during the sixties, a decade of changes both good and bad, that Cicely met the love of her life, Miles Davis. She was briefly introduced to him by a friend. Then Cicely and Miles frequently ran into each other in Central Park. They became friends, then they began dating. He was a gifted, internationally known trumpeter—a brilliant, creative man. He asked Cicely to be the model for his next album cover.

The two fell deeply in love. They became engaged, but at the last minute, without a word to Cicely, Miles married someone else. This was obviously hurtful. But it was also baffling that he acted this way. It was the beginning of Miles showing Cicely how complicated he was. She moved on and concentrated on her career.

The sixties were years of upheaval in America, much of it racial. The Civil Rights Movement was in full swing, and there were assassinations of Martin Luther King Jr., Malcolm X, and presidential candidate Robert Kennedy. People were deeply worried and eager to do something constructive about the violence and uncertainty. Cicely considered how she could help but at first did not know what to do.

Eventually Cicely found her place in the world of civil rights. She decided she would use her acting abilities to present on the screen only true Black women. Positive roles only. No stereotypes. No negative characters. No criminals. It would mean that she would have fewer roles to play. But that's the direction she took.

During the early seventies, a genre of movies became popular that was termed Blaxploitation. This was a merging of the words *Black* and *exploitation*. It meant that movies were being made by Black directors and starring Black actors, which was exciting. Black actors and directors were employed and calling the shots on the big screen.

But Blaxploitation movies were controversial. While many were glad to see more Black people on the screen, the movie plots were usually about Black people living outside the law, with lots of violence and raw language. Black women were presented very unfavorably on the screen. Cicely had made the choice not to be involved in any movie that unfavorably presented Black people onscreen, especially Black women. She did not believe God gave her the gift of acting for such use. She never performed in a Blaxploitation movie. So, in the middle of such a strong film movement, she was often not employed.

But Cicely's career eventually began to take off. She gained a reputation as an excellent actress with integrity. She got a starring role in the 1972 movie *Sounder*, a touching story of a Southern Black family trying to get along as sharecroppers in the Great Depression. Cicely believed in her heart that this part was meant for her, and she threw everything into it. She developed her character, Rebecca, with her own mother and grandmother in mind. It made a powerful impact on the screen.

The reviews were over the moon about this up-and-coming actress named Cicely Tyson. She even earned an Academy Award nomination. She was still a newcomer in movies and did not expect to win (she didn't). But the nomination caused her career to move solidly upward. After that, she acted in many movies in both large and small roles, though she is probably best known for both *Sounder* and a very well received, made-for-television film titled *The Autobiography of Miss Jane Pittman.*

During these years, Miles Davis showed up in her life again. His impulsive marriage had lasted only a year, and now he'd been alone for a long time. Cicely finally agreed to start seeing him again. Why? Because they both felt a deep and loving connection to one another that would last for the rest of their lives, no matter what happened between them. Eventually they married each other.

Soon Cicely could see that Miles was a drug addict. That addiction made him turn into a different person altogether. This was difficult for anyone to live with, and Cicely was a self-described "church girl" who did not drink, smoke, or take drugs. She was a disciplined vegetarian and runner. Living with chaos was very hard for her, especially as she worked. Watching the love of her life slide toward an early death was even harder.

Although Miles Davis loved Cicely, his addiction caused him to mistreat her and eventually abuse and abandon her. Cicely held nothing against Miles, whom she referred to as "a tortured soul." She loved him always. But he finally became dangerous, and she knew she could not be with him any longer. Three years after they stopped living together, Miles died. Cicely never married again.

Cicely continued to act in carefully chosen roles. She was in the very popular films *Roots*, *Fried Green Tomatoes*, *The Help*, and more, plus movies produced by her dear friend, director and actor Tyler Perry. Even in her senior years, she worked consistently.

A thrill for this fine actress was going back to the live stage. She starred as the elderly mother in the stage play *A Trip to Bountiful*. While in her eighties, she had a part in the hit TV series *How to Get Away with Murder*. She never seemed to retire. She earned many awards for her work, the most impressive being three Emmys for her television movies, a Tony for her stage work, and—most thrilling of all—an honorary Oscar for her amazing career.

In 2016, she was awarded the coveted Presidential Medal of Freedom by President Barack Obama. He spoke eloquently about Cicely's career. Then he paused and added, "And she's just gorgeous." In the middle of the laughter and applause that followed, he added matter-of-factly, "Yes, she is."

In January 2021, her autobiography was published, appropriately titled after Cicely's favorite hymn, *Just as I Am*. Two days after it released to the public, Cicely Tyson died in her birthplace of Harlem. She was ninety-seven years old. Friends and family celebrated her life at Abyssinian Baptist Church, where Cicely attended services and where she had a pew dedicated to her beloved mother.

One of the many things Cicely Tyson will be known for is paving the way for great Black actresses to star in, write, and direct movies and television shows. Never had so many Black women appeared on screen in the movies and on television than in the very year Cicely died. In one of her last interviews, Cicely was asked by journalist Gayle King how she would like to be remembered. She paused. Then she smiled and said, "I've done my best. That's all."

Yes, she did. And far more.

LET'S REVIEW

1. Why did Cicely believe she was not beautiful? What factors led her to think this way?
2. Why didn't Cicely's mother want her acting in movies? Why did she change her mind?
3. How many jobs did Cicely work to support her daughter before becoming an actress?

LET'S DO MORE

Cicely chose her own role in the Civil Rights Movement. What was that, and how effective was she? Can you think of causes you're interested in? What's the best way to use your specific talents to make the world better?

(1934–2020)

Civil Rights Movement Mother

"Be yourself, and God will bring you through."

t was the girl's last day of school before spring and summer break. Black students needed to help in the fields, and they wouldn't be back for many months. That was disappointing to the young girl, because she loved going to school in her community's one-room schoolhouse. But in rural Mississippi in the 1940s, most Black children only got through the third grade before dropping out to work. She was already fortunate by having finished the eighth grade. Even though attending high school in her community was rare, she hoped to come back in the late fall.

In school, she had learned about the world beyond the fields of Mississippi—a world where a Black person like herself had some choices. In that outer world, Black children would go to school for most of the year instead of only a few months. They would attend classes in a building that was large and airy and shiny, where books were new and abundant instead of being a few copies of used, tattered castoffs from white schools. She was a student who was eager to learn more and more, and she wanted to get to that world beyond her circumstances someday.

She walked home on this last day of school and helped get supper ready. Later, after the family had eaten and dishes were washed, her mother sat her down and took her hand. "Baby," she said, "I need to tell you something. You won't be going to school anymore. We let you finish out the school term, but we need you working with us full-time."

The girl watched her mother's face and then lowered her eyes. She could see it pained her mother to break this news to her. But she also saw it couldn't be any different. She had gone as far as she could go. Her parents were sharecroppers—picking crops from the property of other people to make a living—and they needed all the paid family workers they could get. An eighth-grade graduate wasn't considered a child anymore. Now she needed to work in the fields and earn money alongside her family. The more they picked, the more money they would have for necessities like food and clothing. School would only be an indulgence from now on—one this family could not afford.

The girl sighed, but she accepted the situation. The very next day, she started picking in the fields with her family. Throughout the long hot days, she let her imagination take her to that outside world she wanted to know. Instead of being sad, she made a decision. If the Good Lord was willing, she would have her own children someday. And those children *would* get an education—a far better one than she could have. That was a promise.

She could have no idea how dangerous keeping that promise would be. Or that her resolve would go down in history.

She was born Lucille Commadore in Tylertown, Mississippi, the daughter of sharecroppers Curtis and Amy Commadore. She grew up helping the family survive by working in the fields alongside her parents. As she ended her teen years, she married Abon Bridges, and they settled in their home in Mississippi to begin raising a family.

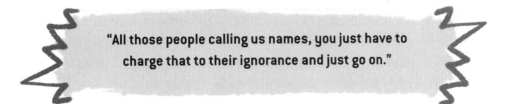

"All those people calling us names, you just have to charge that to their ignorance and just go on."

Once children started coming along, Lucille recalled the promise she'd made to herself long ago—that her children would have the education she was denied. Her children would go beyond the eighth grade. Things would be different for them. Lucille reminded Abon that this was something they needed to attend to. He agreed. They decided to move to New Orleans, where the public school system could offer more to their children.

Schools in New Orleans were segregated, meaning that, by law, schools existed for both white children and Black children, but they were kept separate. Even though New Orleans schools were segregated, and very little money was put into schools for Black students, Lucille knew her children would attend a better school there than they could back home—and they could go on to a proper high school too. That could get them into college. Lucille believed that education was the best way to get away from policies that held Black people back.

When the Bridges moved to New Orleans, they had three of what would eventually be five children—their oldest a girl named Ruby. She attended a segregated school for kindergarten. But while Ruby was on summer break, Lucille learned some big news. The public school system was finally going to integrate. The Supreme Court had heard the case called *Brown v. Board of Education of Topeka*, and they ruled from that case that schools must integrate. So public schools could no longer separate Blacks from whites. Instead, they must offer an equal education in the same buildings, using the same teachers, sharing the same books, Blacks and whites together.

That court decision was made in 1954, the same year Ruby Bridges was born. But Louisiana was one of a few states that did not comply with the decision to integrate public schools. Now, several years later, the federal court had ordered those states to comply.

The New Orleans school district prepared to handle things in their own way. Even though schooling—now to be integrated by law—was a guaranteed right for American children, the school district made Black children take and pass an exam to enter. It was planned to be impossible to pass. However, five children did pass the exam, and one of them was Ruby Bridges.

Friends and neighbors were very proud and happy for Ruby. They came by the house, congratulating and telling Lucille, "She's so smart!" But as the glow of that success started to fade, reality set in. Would these white educators really allow Ruby to attend school? What was that going to look like? Would it be too dangerous?

Lucille and Abon talked this over at great length. They knew Ruby attending an integrated school was the first step in making certain their children—and other Black children—could have the option to go to good schools. But should they subject their child to this uncertain situation? Abon was especially hesitant. He was sure there would be trouble. Lucille also suspected there might be trouble, but she felt this opportunity was so important that they should follow through. She believed she and Abon could help Ruby handle whatever came her way. Abon finally agreed.

This was 1960, during the middle of the Civil Rights Movement in America, a time when people had been actively protesting on behalf of Black people's rights and dignity for many decades. Fast-forward three years to 1963 for a moment, when civil rights leaders would become frustrated with what seemed to be a growing lack of participation in the movement. Those leaders decided to make a radical move—they would allow children and teens to protest on the streets instead of only adults. Those young ones gathered and marched peacefully. In return, they were sprayed with firehoses, beaten with clubs, and attacked by huge dogs. A horrified world would see that on television, and this would reinvigorate the movement. That part of the movement would become known as the Children's Crusade.

But that was later. Ruby was going to school in 1960, three years before the Children's Crusade. This little girl was doing this solo. Her parents had reason to be afraid. Two other Black children were to attend the same school with her, but their parents withdrew them for the very reasons that concerned the Bridges. Yes, they had support from their neighbors and their church, but what about the rest of the town? And would the white police keep Ruby safe?

In the end, the Bridges let their daughter attend the newly integrated school. Ruby was enrolled in the first grade and became the first Black child—the *only* Black child that school year—to attend all-white William Frantz Elementary School in New Orleans and get the same education as white children.

Preparations kicked in at Lucille's home for the big event. She and Abon stressed to Ruby that she should present herself in a well-behaved and dignified manner. A supporter from the north donated beautiful dresses and shoes for little Ruby to wear to school. Neighbors brought in food and made plans to babysit the younger children at home when Lucille would be away escorting Ruby.

Dad Abon also wanted to escort and protect his family. But Lucille knew that having Abon, a Black man, present would make some white people more tense and potentially violent. A mother and daughter might be given more grace than an adult Black man. Abon reluctantly agreed to stay away.

The day before school started, Lucille and Abon were invited to meet with the superintendent. He asked if they were praying people. They said they were. He said, "You'll need to pray all you can, because this is going to get rough." But before he made his suggestion, there was already plenty of prayer going on, both at church and at home. Lucille continued teaching Ruby Bible verses to memorize—words and phrases to bolster and comfort her.

On November 14, 1960, cars full of federal marshals drove to the Bridges home to transport Ruby to school. As neighbors watched, Ruby stepped out of the house, hand in hand with Lucille. Ruby wore a lovely starched dress and shined shoes and pretty socks. Four very tall armed men with gold armbands escorted them to a waiting car. They drove away with other cars full of armed men ahead and behind them.

The cars drove the five blocks to the school, and as they grew closer, crowds of angry white people tried to stand in the way. The cars moved slowly through and stopped at the front steps of the school. As Lucille stepped out, she heard the chants: "Two, four, six, eight, we don't want to integrate!" Over and over. She reached for little Ruby's hand. The four marshals flanked them, in front and behind. "Don't look behind you," one of the marshals said. "Just keep walking. We're right here."

The marshals' one task was to keep Ruby safe. And they did. Crowds of white people screamed at them. They pointed at Ruby and threatened to kill her, calling her vile names. They threw eggs and tomatoes at her. But the marshals never let anything land on Ruby and Lucille, and they kept them moving forward. Sometimes the protests became especially violent and had to be broken up by local police.

Boxed in by the four marshals, Lucille and Ruby walked the gauntlet of angry, screaming people. When they reached the front door of the school, local policemen barred their way. One policeman informed them that, by the governor's order, they could not come in. A federal marshal replied, "The President of the United States says we can." That did it. The police stepped aside.

Indoors, Lucille and Ruby were escorted to the principal's office, where they spent her entire first day amid a lot of chaos. From the office windows, they watched parents come to the school and yank their children away. Five hundred white children left school that first day because their parents did not want them to be educated alongside one Black student.

The next day, the school decided that Ruby would have a teacher to herself in an otherwise empty classroom. Many of the teachers had resigned already over this turn of events, and only one who was still there volunteered to be Ruby's teacher. She was Barbara Henry, a white woman from Boston. She was an excellent teacher, and Lucille was relieved to see that she was also a caring human being.

Barbara Henry handled the classroom as if it were perfectly normal to have only one student and the sounds of screaming crowds on the other side of the walls. Amid all the racket outside, she taught Ruby reading and math, and sometimes the two played games together. Ruby would be her only student all year, and the teacher later would say what a joy it was every day to work with Ruby as her student. Eventually parents brought their children back, since there was not really any other school option for them, but Ruby was kept apart from them in Barbara Henry's classroom until summer break.

Meanwhile, the marshals stayed on site. They escorted Ruby to and from the bathroom. Because so many in the crowd threatened to poison the child, the marshals only let her eat what Lucille packed for her. Of course, the school had already determined she could not eat or play with the others, claiming it was too dangerous for her. So day after day, Ruby did everything with only her teacher in the classroom and marshals nearby in the hallway.

When each school day was over, Mom Lucille was there. She and the four marshals walked Ruby out of the building and to the car. Several marshals' vehicles drove them home, often followed by lines of honking cars filled with screaming white people. Once they got to the Bridges's street, Black neighbors came outside to line the street, and the white people's cars turned around.

Weeks into the school year, Lucille learned that on that first day, a man in the crowd had pulled a gun. His plan was to shoot Lucille. His logic was that if the mother was dead, the child would not go to school. Fortunately, he was disarmed and arrested. Since things were stressful enough, the marshals chose not to share this information with Lucille for a while.

One day outside the school, protesters carried a child's coffin. It was open, and they had placed a black doll in it, to show Lucille what it would be like if her child were killed. Photos exist of this. In it, a crowd of adults carry the coffin, laughing. Little Ruby was very frightened by this, and she had nightmares about it for years, dreaming that the coffin had wings and flew around her bed at night. It took a while for those nightmares to calm down.

For all of her first-grade year, amid rage and death threats from the street and sidewalks, Ruby Bridges was escorted to and from school by Lucille and four armed federal marshals. Every day. Neighbors stayed protective, and a group of them walked behind the slow-moving marshals' vehicles every morning, showing their support. Each night the federal marshals guarded the street outside the Bridges home with machine guns. All so that a six-year-old Black girl could attend school.

Ruby never missed a day. Which meant Lucille never missed a day either.

During the early days of Ruby's school attendance, a white stranger driving into town saw the crowds. He pulled over to see what all the fuss was about. Since this man was not a local, he found someone on the sidewalk to fill him in. Then he saw Ruby and Lucille being led up the school steps by federal marshals.

This stranger was Dr. Robert Coles, and he was a child psychiatrist. He felt immediate concern for Ruby's welfare when he saw the anger in the crowd. He contacted Lucille and offered his services for free as a children's therapist to support Ruby during this trying time.

The Bridges accepted his offer, and Dr. Coles met with Ruby once a week in her home. He was amazed at how well adjusted she was, even after months of being verbally attacked and threatened by frightening people every single day. Lucille and Abon, he observed, were wise and humble people who had committed themselves to keeping life as normal as possible for their daughter in this strange time. He was impressed at the passages of Scripture they had committed to memory, which they shared with their daughter.

Most importantly, Dr. Coles observed that Ruby's parents had taught her not to hate those people yelling at her but instead to pray for them. When he asked Ruby what she prayed when the crowds were so mean, she told him, "Please, dear God, forgive them because they don't know what they're doing." Dr. Coles was very impressed and even in awe over the way Lucille and Abon parented their child. He later wrote extensively about that year and what he observed.

Because of Ruby's involvement in integrating her school, Abon lost his job. Then Lucille lost her job. Local grocery stores refused to sell to Lucille. Even Ruby's sharecropper grandparents were evicted from their long-time home.

But many more people were supportive of the family. A neighbor found a new job for Abon. Other neighbors provided food, babysitting, and emotional support in countless ways. The beautiful clothes little

Ruby wore that were photographed so often by the press were donated by someone Lucille didn't even know at the time.

Eventually the public schools in New Orleans were fully integrated. Lucille was grateful that first year had ended with everyone still on their feet. All that trouble paid off—her children and other Black children received their education. Ruby went on to college. As the kids were becoming adults, Abon died in 1978. Eventually Lucille became a grandmother. And life went on.

But 2005 was a horrific year for Lucille. Her grandson—Ruby's eldest child—was murdered in random violence in New Orleans at age seventeen. Only weeks later, Hurricane Katrina hit. New Orleans had seen many hurricanes, but this one devastated the levee system that kept the surrounding waters at bay. The majority of New Orleans flooded, including the area where Lucille lived. Many lives were lost. Lucille, like many other citizens, was evacuated to Houston. Her home was ruined, so she stayed in Houston for several years.

Lucille finally returned to New Orleans around 2015, and she died there in 2020 at age eighty-six. On that day, Ruby Bridges posted on social media a black-and-white photo of Lucille Bridges holding her little daughter's hand as they descended the school steps, surrounded by federal marshals. Ruby wrote, "Today our country lost a hero. Brave, progressive, a champion for change. She helped alter the course of so many lives by setting me out on my path as a six-year-old little girl. Our nation lost a Mother of the Civil Rights Movement today. And I lost my mom. I love you and am grateful for you. May you rest in peace."

History remembers young Ruby Bridges integrating her New Orleans school. A famous painting exists of that first day. Illustrator Norman Rockwell, best-known for painting cheery themes about mostly white

Americans for the covers of *The Saturday Evening Post*, re-created the scene of Ruby being escorted down a hall by four marshals in gold armbands. They march in step past walls smeared with tomatoes and ugly words. It's called *The Problem We All Live With*. *Look* magazine used it on their cover. It was controversial at the time but is now considered a masterpiece of sorts. A copy of this painting hangs in the offices of most federal marshals to this day.

Much is made of little Ruby Bridges's courage in the face of mobs of hateful people—and rightly so. But truly not enough is remembered about the courage and the selflessness of her mother, Lucille. Ruby would never have attended school without her mother's strong influence, and during that first year she had Lucille's full, daily support.

Imagine how difficult it was for Lucille as a mother, to watch potentially dangerous adults act so horribly toward her little girl. Imagine watching that small coffin with a doll lying in it carried down the street by laughing people. Imagine how Lucille had to temper her protective instincts and choose to trust the marshals—and ultimately God.

Interviews of this brave, soft-spoken woman can be found online. She talks about how much she believes in education and how one can be anything one wants to be if educated. She says she was glad to be part of the movement to make that happen for other Black children.

And we are glad for all you did, Mrs. Bridges.

LET'S REVIEW

1. How did segregation in the school system show itself? What was it like for Black students?
2. Why did the Bridges family move to New Orleans?

3. In what ways was Dr. Coles amazed by Lucille and Abon Bridges as Ruby's parents?

LET'S DO MORE

Find a copy of the Norman Rockwell painting *The Problem We All Live With*. It's about Ruby's walk into school with the federal marshals. Though not all the details in the painting are accurate, the mood of the painting is. What parts of the painting are most powerful to you?

aNN atwateR

(1935–2016)

Community Activist

"Whatever you believe in, stand on it, baby—stand on it."

She was one of nine children in a Black family that was very poor. She was born during the Great Depression, when many people lived in desperate poverty. Her father made only five cents an hour, a terribly low wage even for Depression-era workers, so all the children pitched in to help make more. As early as she could remember, she was working in fields with her sharecropper family.

Sometimes the owner of the farm would feed a meal to the workers. As a Black person, the child was required to go to the back door of the house to receive her lunch. But first the white workers were given their meals. That was the unspoken and understood rule. Once the white workers finished, the Black workers ate what was left.

As a little girl, she learned to accept this. But unfortunately, she also accepted something else that came with it—a belief that as a Black person she was not important. That she always came second, if at all.

That message showed up everywhere in her limited world. She observed it when her mother took her to the store to buy a few groceries or to a white farmer's home to negotiate work. Whatever white person her mother dealt with would keep his or her distance by standing a couple yards away and shouting at her. There was no normal conversation like when white people spoke to each other. Her mother was yelled at as if she were stupid. To get what she needed for the family, her mother had to remain polite and soft-spoken in these situations. The child could see that, as Black people, they were powerless. She lived under that cloud for years.

Then one day she was in a situation that proved otherwise. That day she realized the same God who made white people made her. It was a powerful revelation that made all the difference. That's when things began to change inside her, and this led to change around her. She learned to speak up for herself. One day, she spoke up for someone else. Then she spoke up for many others who could not find their voices. She decided God had given her the gift of speaking up.

She never stopped speaking up.

And over the years, she got louder.

———

Ann Atwater was born in 1935 in Hallsboro, North Carolina, to share-cropper parents. Her mother died when Ann was only six. Ann and her eight brothers and sisters worked the fields alongside the adults to make enough to eat and house the family. Her father was a deacon in the church, and this is where Ann gained her faith and started developing the self-confidence she would draw on later in life.

Like many girls in her day, Ann married too young. She was thirteen when she married a boy named French and fourteen when she had their first child, a girl. They moved to Durham, North Carolina. Her new husband was a few years older than she was, but he really was still a boy himself inside. He could not handle the responsibility of a wife and child, and after the first baby was born, he abandoned the family. He eventually returned, but after their second daughter was born, he abandoned the family for good.

> "All of our blood, when it comes out, is the same color. I haven't seen any blood different yet than the color of mine."

Still a teenager, now Ann was stranded in Durham, far away from family, trying to survive with two small children. She got a job as a housemaid and was paid less than other maids in town simply because she had no idea what to charge. When she was between housecleaning jobs, she figured out how to stretch whatever food she had, feeding her girls and herself mostly cabbage, fatback, and rice, sometimes for days at a time. She lived in horrible rental houses in a falling-down Black neighborhood called Hayti.

Hayti had deplorable living conditions—bad enough that one out of every three Black babies born there died in their first year. The majority of Black adults died in Hayti before age forty. The houses were often shacks sitting on muddy roads. Most had no indoor plumbing, which meant using outhouses in unhealthy conditions. Landlords chose not to fix things.

Ann had that landlord problem. The three-room house she rented had running water, but the bathtub had collapsed into the rotted wood floor, and the toilet, when it was flushed, gushed a geyser of water toward the ceiling. Ann would stomp her foot on the floor to turn on the porch light, and she stomped it again to turn it off. Even this potential fire hazard was ignored by the landlord.

One day Ann approached social services for some help. Her doctor had insisted she pay attention to her health and not work so hard. She still worked but not as much, and she needed to make ends meet. Her rent was behind by one month, and the landlord planned to evict her and her two small children. As she explained the problem to two white welfare workers, she watched them literally laugh at her. It was demoralizing. When Ann left, she felt an anger she'd never had before. She found herself hating white people.

A couple of days later, there was a knock on her door. Two community activists, a Black man and woman, wondered if she needed anything they could help with. Ann had no idea what these two young people thought they could do for her, but she showed them what was wrong—and dangerous—about her house and explained that the landlord planned to evict her. The young man said they'd drum up money for the back rent. But he believed they should also talk to the landlord first, and that she and they should do it together. In the meantime, would she be willing to come to a community activist meeting that night?

Ann said she'd come to a dozen meetings if it helped her, though she expected it would not. She began attending meetings intended to organize the poor Blacks in Hayti so that they could have better living conditions. In the meantime, she watched the two activists who came to her house reason with her landlord. They agreed to pay the back rent after he fixed the problems in the house. To Ann's shock, the landlord agreed. The landlord did a subpar job of fixing things, but he did some improving, and he did wait for that back rent. And she was not evicted.

This was the first time Ann had ever seen such a thing—the powerless exerting power. It was the beginning of a new way of thinking for Ann, a high school dropout and single mother. She began taking classes in community action activities, and she learned she was good at some things that had never occurred to her. She read well and understood well. She could express herself to a roomful of people. She had an interest in housing, hers and her neighbors', so that's where she put her energies first.

Ann also began to realize who she was at her very core. That person inside had a strong sense of justice. She also had a temper, and it would get her into trouble if she didn't rein it in. And yet not reining it in could also be successful. People needed to see her righteous anger sometimes to know she meant business.

It should also be noted that Ann was a large woman. She was tall and very heavyset. She spoke with passion—she had a big voice that carried—and people took notice. If she wasn't being heard, she would do things like position herself in doorways so that nobody would get past her. Literally, due to her size, nobody *could* get past her. Once Ann realized she could use even her size to her advantage, she did just that.

The odd thing about being a large, Black woman in Durham was that it made her socially invisible to whites. Ann decided to take advantage of that too. She showed up in public meetings, sat in the back, and learned so much. Then she even showed up at private meetings and sat through those. How did she do this? White people did not notice the large Black woman sitting at the back of the room. Or if they did notice her, they figured she was the cleaning woman, resting her feet.

Oh, the things Ann learned by simply watching and listening. She discovered how local governments worked. She became knowledgeable by literally hiding in plain sight. She also shared what she learned with her activist friends. Sometimes white committee members would get upset with each other because they believed someone among them was leaking information. But it was Ann, sharing what she'd learned by sitting right in front of them.

In 1954, the Supreme Court made the case in *Brown v. Board of Education of Topeka* that public schools must be integrated throughout the land, including the South. But living out that decision locally often stalled because white policy makers wanted to keep integration at bay for as long as possible. In some places in the South, including the city of Durham, schools were still segregated years after the decision.

This had ramifications. Not only did Black schools operate with hand-me-downs and lack of supplies, but the school buildings were not always safe to house children. There was no money allotted from the government to take care of Black schools and their students. As Ann had clearly seen when she was a girl, Black children were treated as second-class citizens or worse.

By 1971, seventeen years after the Supreme Court ruling, Durham's public schools were still segregated. The city council—segregationists all—finally decided they would allow the local community to decide how and if it would integrate. Just because it was a federal law didn't mean the city would comply. But they did feel the community itself could make that decision. They started what was called a charrette.

Charrette is a French word meaning a community summit where citizens join in discussions over a short period of time on either side of a decision until they can vote on it. In Durham, the city council said they would abide by the charrette's decision on whether to integrate the schools. Ann was encouraged to be part of it.

Ann had been busy working on community improvements for many years by now. She was fierce in action and successful at getting policies changed for Black citizens. She was known to say, "I will not take no for an answer. I have to have the word *yes.*"

In Ann's civil rights organizing around town, she often heard angry comments directed toward her by whites. She didn't care. She knew she was doing God's work. And she also didn't care because she hated white people. Yes, she was a church-loving Christian, but at that time she still would be the first to tell someone that she hated white people.

Ann noticed one white man in town who seemed especially hateful toward her, so she always kept an eye on him. Eventually she would learn that his name was C. P. Ellis, and he was the president of the local Ku Klux Klan. C. P. had grown up poor and powerless even as a white person in Durham. Often that was the kind of person who was attracted to the KKK. He felt a sense of belonging there, even if they were united only by hatred for Blacks. He moved through the ranks to become president, and that meant everything to him.

If Ann noticed him as a possible threat, he felt the same about her. Her loud voice and large presence were intimidating, though he'd never acknowledge that. When he threw a racial slur at her, she lobbed one right back. This was new to the Klansman. The woman showed no fear. C. P. once saw her get angry at a white councilman who had swiveled his chair around so that his back was to her, his way of saying he wasn't listening. Ann marched up and physically spun his chair back around and told him to his face he was going to listen to her. And he did.

Both Ann and C. P. decided to attend city council meetings that discussed the new possibility of integrating the schools so that they could have a say. Ann wanted integrated schools because her daughters were getting subpar educations in a school with a decrepit building that received no funds to better the situation. C. P. did not want integrated schools because he considered Blacks inferior to whites, and he didn't want his children mixing with them.

In a twist that seemed like it could only be in a movie, Black activist Ann Atwater and Klan president C. P. Ellis were chosen by the council to cochair the two sides of discussion in the newly formed charrette. No one was more surprised than they were. At first they refused. They were simply not going to work with someone they hated, and that was that. But they were finally persuaded to give it a try for the sake of the community both cared about—and for their own school-aged children.

The series of charrette meetings began. At first Ann and C. P. would get so angry with each other that the other members felt certain it would go nowhere. The two fought and yelled at each other. They had a very hard time speaking civilly to each other at all. Sometimes they needed a referee! Other members were concerned, because if the cochairs couldn't get along, what good was this? Then something happened that caused change to come.

Both C. P. and Ann frequently received death threats by phone. Now their children were getting flak from other kids at school—and even some teachers—about what their parents were doing in the charrette.

C. P. phoned Ann. He said, "Look, I don't like you, and you don't like me. But we got to do something because our kids are suffering in school. If this thing is gonna be a success, you and I are gonna have to make it one. Can we lay aside some of these feelings?"

Ann said yes, she was willing to try. But inside, she still didn't trust him.

The charrette invited the public to attend its meetings. Ann and C. P. managed to be civil toward one another for most of the ten days they met. The work lasted twelve hours a day and was exhausting.

One day after a meeting, C. P. saw Ann sitting by herself in a room with a few others in it. He sat down beside her. Ann was surprised, but they both started chatting like normal people with one another. This turned to talk of their kids, and they both shared that their children were getting harassed at school over the charrette. Ann and C. P. both started to see how alike they were instead of how different. They both loved and wanted to protect their children. Why were they doing this if not for the kids?

This led to them talking about how they had both grown up in such severe poverty. Ann shared about being too poor to own a doll, so she'd made one out of grass using roots for hair. C. P. was stunned. He'd watched his sister do the same thing when they were kids.

Suddenly, C. P. began to weep. Now it was Ann who was stunned. By now the room was empty of everyone else. Ann said nothing at first, then she took the hand of the white Klansman she had deeply hated. She gently soothed him, saying, "It's okay. It's okay . . ." until she too began to weep. Ann Atwater and C. P. Ellis sat together and cried and, on the spot, forged a deep friendship—a kinship, really.

In one of the final charrette meetings, Durham students, both Black and white, told the committee they wanted to attend school together. That made several members of the charrette take notice. In the end, the charrette members—including C. P.—voted to integrate, though not by a landslide. C. P. publicly resigned from the Klan because he simply no longer hated Black people. And Ann no longer hated white people. She would say, "God gave me the gift to reach out and touch." And that's what she continued to do.

Ann and C. P. were interviewed by journalist Studs Terkel for his book *Race.* From there, people learned about these unassuming, small-town heroes. Magazine articles were written about them. A play about their friendship was written and performed. A documentary was made. Eventually a Hollywood movie was released, with Ann beautifully played by renowned actress Taraji P. Henson. Ann gave her enthusiastic blessing to that casting.

Ann Atwater and C. P. Ellis remained extremely close friends until he died in 2005. His funeral was a private one, for family only—and Ann Atwater. The Ellis family invited her to give the eulogy.

On the day of the funeral, Ann arrived early to spend some time next to her friend's casket. Nobody else had arrived yet. The undertaker quietly approached her. He kept his voice down, as undertakers do. "I'm sorry," he said, "but this funeral is for Mr. Claiborne Ellis."

Ann acknowledged that she knew that.

The now uncomfortable man said, "This service is for family members only."

Ann acknowledged that she knew that too.

"Well," he continued, "are you a family member?"

Ann said that she was.

Completely flummoxed, the man pressed on. "May I ask how you are related to the deceased?"

Ann paused and gave the man her famous glare. Then she slowly stretched out her response: "C. P. was my brother."

Truly, that was the miracle of Ann Atwater's life. Her sworn enemy—a white former Klansman—had become her beloved brother. Her anger had drained away, replaced by peace. Of the many awards she won as an activist by the time she died in 2016, it was that peace—one that fed her friendship with C. P.—that mattered most.

LET'S REVIEW

1. Describe the things that happened to Ann when she was young that caused her to believe she was a second-class citizen.

2. Where was Hayti? What was wrong with Ann's three-room house there?

3. What kinds of things did Ann learn by sitting in plain sight at meetings?

LET'S DO MORE

Ann herself claimed that she hated white people for a long time. Think about how that impacted her life. How did she get past it? Do you hate any person? Any groups? How might you get past this? Could you learn to love this person or group? What would it take to do that? Write about it in your journal if you keep one, or write an essay or poem about these feelings.

MARVA COLLINS

(1936–2015)

Educator

"People predict. You determine."

er father was one of the wealthiest Black men in their Alabama town, and she was his only child. Although she was born during the Great Depression, it had little effect on her life. She spent her early childhood living with her parents in a six-bedroom home filled with fine furniture and thick rugs. She had lovely, store-bought dresses to wear at a time when other little Black girls in town were wearing dresses made from reused flour sacks. She even had her very own horse.

Her father was not educated, but he was the smartest man around and a whiz at business. He owned several businesses and a thousand-acre cattle ranch. All of this was highly unusual for a Black man in the 1930s South. People came to him for financial help—not just Black people but white people too.

And yet all the respect her father commanded and all the wealth he made could not change something very important for his daughter—her education. In the segregated South, schooling for Black students was barely supported by the local school boards. Teachers in those Black schools seldom had any training or higher education. The school this little girl attended was in an unpainted wood building with only two rooms. Its few desks were beat up, and the smaller children sat two to a seat. There were books, but not many, and none of them were even close to being new. During lessons, students shared their books. Sometimes everyone in each room did the same lesson, no matter their age or grade. Or students who had already learned a lesson helped instruct the younger ones.

The building had few windows. There was a woodstove in each room, and in chilly months, parents sent wood to school with their children to burn in the stove for heat. The bathroom was an outhouse behind the building, and hands were washed at an outdoor pump.

From the outside, this school was certainly lacking in comforts and resources. But what this school did have was plenty of teacher dedication, plenty of an infectious love of learning, and plenty of hope.

The little rich girl found her true place in the world in that shabby building, thanks to the responsible and loving teachers she knew there. She took that desire to learn with her into the world, and when she grew up, she knew she wanted to help children—all children—develop the love of learning she had. She came to believe that education mattered almost more than anything. So she chose to teach.

All that two-room-schoolhouse togetherness and love of learning were going to come in very handy for this teacher who would eventually become revered and famous.

For what?

For her ability to teach the unteachable.

Marva Delores Knight was born in 1936 in Monroeville, Alabama—not far from Mobile—and was the only child of Henry and Bessie Knight. Her family was wealthy and powerful in the Black community. She lacked for nothing. This was particularly noticeable because she was born into the Great Depression, a time when many Americans were desperately poor. She saw how others lived, and she saw the

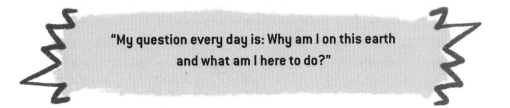

"My question every day is: Why am I on this earth and what am I here to do?"

difference. Perhaps this is what made her care so much in later years for poorer children.

Marva was especially close to her father, and she spent much of her early childhood time with him. She admired him greatly, and he adored his only child. He was tall and strong and fearless. Daddy kept Marva by his side all the time, driving her around town with him in his black Cadillac. In many ways, he treated her like he might have treated a son. She observed his actions in his businesses and sat with him in dealmaking meetings. She saw how even white people came to him to borrow money.

Marva's daddy liked to remind his daughter how smart she was, and this gave her confidence in herself from an early age. Her mother, on the other hand, was very critical of her daughter, often impatient with her and shooing her out of the house. Nevertheless, Marva chose to believe that her mother's response to her probably made her want to achieve more. She also determined not to do some things her mother's way. For example, Marva would one day be affectionate and open with her children in ways her mother seemed unable to be.

Daddy read with Marva every night, stories from Aesop's fables or newspapers and magazines. She learned to read before she went to school, and this was mostly because of her grandmother, whom she called Mama-Dear. The kind and patient Mama-Dear read aloud to Marva from the Bible. Marva loved the musical language of the Scriptures. Mama-Dear also recited from memory long poems like "Hiawatha" or "Paul Revere's Ride."

When Marva was only nine years old and already an avid reader, an aunt introduced her to Shakespeare. Marva fell in love with all of it. She memorized poetry and lines from Shakespeare, and one day would use that technique of memorizing beautiful language with the children she taught.

Until she turned twelve, Marva's childhood was carefree and happy. Then her parents separated. Nothing was explained to her when her father moved to one town and she and her mother moved to another town, Atmore. But her childhood changed dramatically.

She would always remember those earlier years in Monroeville. As it is with many people, early childhood carved Marva into the strong adult she would become. She carried on with less interaction with her father. She grew up to be tall and straight in stature like him, and she carried herself in her father's regal way.

Although nobody in Marva's family was well educated, she attended Clark College. She graduated in 1957 with a degree in secretarial sciences, which many college women earned then. It was considered practical at a time when few occupations were open to women. She taught secretarial skills for two years, though she had not really planned on teaching. She felt some uncertainty about what to do with her life.

Like many young people in the 1950s, Marva moved north to Chicago for more opportunity. While working as a medical secretary in Chicago, she met a young draftsman named Clarence Collins. They fell in love. About the same time, she also began working in the public school system as a substitute teacher. She paused teaching to marry Clarence in 1960, and they had three children in a matter of several years: Eric, Patrick, and Cynthia. The family purchased a brownstone house in West Garfield Park. They lived on the ground floor and rented out the upstairs floor.

While the children were still young, Marva went back to work, this time as a full-time substitute teacher in the Chicago public schools. But she found its education system lacking. She felt it suffered from no discipline, no expectations of students, no resources, and ultimately, very bad test scores. This especially impacted low-income Black children.

Marva was outspoken about her views on the school system's failures. This did not make her any friends at work. In fact, her coworkers tended to stay away from her. But Marva believed there was a better way to educate. She was appalled at the educational and behavioral labels children were given, how badly they did on tests, and how easily people gave up on them. Many schools today offer benefits to children with learning disabilities, but at that time Marva was not seeing much help for these students beyond naming the problem. She was especially shocked at how many could not even read. And she was not pleased with her own children's education, either. After fourteen years of observing and teaching, she decided to act.

Marva discussed it with her husband, and they decided to start their own school. They pulled the money they needed out of Marva's pension, and, in 1975, Marva opened a private school in the upstairs of the Collins family's brownstone home. She named it Westside Preparatory Academy. She started with a handful of students—two of her own children and a few other students who had been labeled "learning disabled."

Marva's school charged a tuition, but it wasn't much—and usually wasn't enough. The financial struggles were mighty at first. Marva was the sole teacher for a long time, seating grades kindergarten through eighth grade in one large room with her. She taught all ages at once and was very hands-on in her classroom. When some children caught on to lessons earlier than others, she encouraged them to "give back" by helping other children. This came from the small schoolhouse method of her childhood—lots of students in one room and lots of interaction with the teacher, with older kids sometimes teaching the younger ones.

The room was completely focused on Marva as she taught her lesson—and often deviated from it when she knew doing so would benefit the students. Tall and impeccably dressed, she was on her feet all day in that classroom, moving around, leaning over the children at their desks, writing on the chalkboard, insisting students come up and write on the board too or read aloud from their seats. Her technique was to be firm and loving at the same time, and she openly expressed her encouragement and affection. If a student needed more help, she met with her or him an hour before school started. One of her many mottos was, "There is a brilliant child locked inside every student." She showed that to be true when, after the first year, every one of her students' scores on standardized tests increased by five grades or more.

This was unheard of. Such victories with working with the supposedly unteachable or the learning disabled certainly got attention. Marva would eventually be termed a "miracle worker." But her response to that was, "I'm a teacher. A teacher is someone who leads. There is no magic here. I do not walk on water. I do not part the sea. I just love children."

Many people observed her, and all would walk away marveling at how this brilliant and caring woman held the attention of the students and said loving things to them at the same time. Children used the phonics system to learn to read, sounding out syllables and words and understanding their roots. Marva had them reading Shakespeare aloud—and loving it. Students in all grades wrote a composition every day. They had to memorize a poem every week. They read the newspapers daily, and they were required to read books outside of the lessons. They built strong vocabularies.

She also taught students self-respect, reminding them that, "Character is what you know you are, not what others think you have." She enjoyed sharing fun and intriguing word play, like: "Mr. Meant-To has a friend, his name is Didn't-Do. Have you met them? They live together in a house called Never-Win. I am told it is haunted by the Ghost of Might-Have-Been." And children responded.

Some of her students were average in ability, sent to Marva so they could develop what talents they had. Some were brilliant but were being ignored in a system that did not help them at their own level. Many had learning disabilities—real or assumed—that caused them to fail in school. Many had behavioral problems that got them kicked out of school. Marva said to every one of them, "I will never let you fail." She always made good on that promise.

Word got around. Educators shadowed her to learn what she knew. Reporters with notebooks and cameras showed up. The CBS television show *60 Minutes* loved Marva—they covered her success, then years later came back to report on the children who had appeared in that first show. Those remarkable interviews of children can be seen online.

Due to Marva's popularity, a made-for-television movie was made about her. It aired in 1981. Cicely Tyson was chosen to play Marva in this biography, called *The Marva Collins Story*, and Morgan Freeman played her husband. Tyson, a highly celebrated actress, was excited to help bring Marva's story to the screen, and she spent a lot of time with Marva to understand her character.

At first, Marva insisted on being on the set every day, which soon became difficult for the actress playing her. Tyson understood that Marva wanted her situation presented authentically. It became apparent, however, that Marva needed tight control, which thwarted some of the art of acting.

The director apparently quietly spoke to Marva, and halfway through rehearsals, Marva decided to trust the process—and the award-winning actress playing her. Marva stopped showing up. Everyone breathed a little easier and went about their good work. The picture was so well done that Cicely Tyson was nominated for an Emmy for her performance.

The next year, in 1982, Marva's book, *Marva Collins' Way: Returning to Excellence in Education*, coauthored with Civia Tamarkin, was published. The famous author of *Roots*, Alex Haley, chose to write the foreword to the book, which was a way of introducing Marva to the reader. *Marva Collins' Way* offered personal information about her in her own words, and it also showed readers how she taught and how to use her methods. It was an inspiring book.

Then an unusual thing happened. In 1983, a twenty-three-year-old college basketball player contacted her. His name was Kevin Ross, and he was a student at Creighton University. He had made it to his senior year of college on an athletic scholarship—but he could not read. He was increasingly frustrated and embarrassed by this, so he contacted Marva to be his teacher.

Ross enrolled at Westside Prep, in the second grade. The college basketball player showed up every day, tucking his big athlete's body into a child's desk, learning lessons with the other children, and receiving extra tutoring on the side from Marva. By the time he graduated from college the following year, Kevin Ross could read. He and Marva remained friends for the rest of her life.

Marva's accomplishments were noticed by President Ronald Reagan, who wanted her to be his secretary of education. This was certainly an honor, but she chose to decline. The same thing happened when President George H. W. Bush invited her to be his secretary of education. Marva turned down both presidents because she felt her mission was to teach and directly impact students face-to-face, not work as a bureaucrat.

Westside Prep grew. More children needed the attention they could get from this exceptional teacher, so Marva expanded her school. She moved it out of her house and into a building in the West Garfield business district. She trained a few other teachers in her specific techniques and eventually expanded enrollment to up to two hundred students. Marva and her staff continued to teach and inspire kids for many years.

Clarence Collins died in 1995. Their marriage had lasted thirty-five years and was a strong partnership of love and mutual support. Marva and her daughter Cynthia continued to run the school until 2008, when it closed. That same year, this beloved daughter died at age thirty-nine. She left behind an eight-year-old child who moved in with her grandmother. Marva, who now was seventy-two, gladly raised her for the next several years.

Over her lifetime, Marva Collins won many awards and received many honors. But one of the most surprising honors she received was from Prince, the late rock star who was at his peak in popularity in the eighties. Prince spread his tremendous wealth to causes he believed in, and he did this quietly. He was so impressed with Marva's school that, in 1989, he donated $500,000 to help her with it. Then he placed Marva in his music video *The Most Beautiful Girl in the World*. This song and video honored women from many walks of life, and he included Marva as part of his vision for "beautiful." There was mutual respect between the two.

Marva Collins died in June 2015 in South Carolina at age seventy-eight. Hundreds of her former students today live happy and productive lives because of what and how Marva taught them.

Imagine Marva Collins for a moment as a beautiful stone thrown into the middle of a pond. Imagine the circles of ripples extending out from where the stone hit the water. We could find how many students were directly affected by Marva, but we'll never know how many more people were in turn affected by those students. This is how Marva made her mark. Her wisdom and skills live on beyond her—and well beyond those hundreds of students who remember that kind and elegant teacher leaning over their shoulder, encouraging them with just a bit of Alabama honey in her voice, saying, "I *know* you can do it!"

LET'S REVIEW

1. Marva's father was successful even as a Black man in the Depression-era South. How did that show? Name several ways.
2. What were some reasons Marva thought public schools were failing?
3. Who played Marva in the movie about her?

LET'S DO MORE

Marva found creative ways to teach reading to all kinds of learners. Think of something you know how to do well. How would you teach that to another person? Try teaching it together with a friend.

GWEN IFILL

(1955–2016)

Journalist

"You can be the person who turns toward, not away from, the chance to rise above the fray."

She was bright and confident and happy. She loved school. She especially loved words. At twelve years old, she read voraciously and wrote articles and stories. She joined in spirited discussions with her siblings and cousins, all exuberant fast talkers like she was. She was a whiz at Scrabble.

Her immigrant father from Panama so believed in the American system that he insisted his children know what was going on in the world around them. Consequently, the girl and her five siblings had a daily menu of news. Crowded around the family television, they watched NBC's *The Today Show* every morning. School or no school, they each read two daily newspapers. At night after supper, the family landed back in the living room to watch *The Huntley-Brinkley Report* on NBC. Then they talked about it all.

The girl was blessed with curiosity. She drank in information with gusto, becoming a true news junkie. She found herself drawn to the excitement of politics and the anticipation of a new president and possibilities. Later she would laughingly call herself a "nerd" because, even at an early age, she relished watching the presidential conventions of both parties on television with her family. Her folks always let the kids stay up late on election night to see who won.

But she observed something perplexing. Very seldom would this girl see anybody on television who looked like her. Almost never did she see Black people. And certainly not in the world of news. Everyone was male. And everyone was white.

Until Melba Tolliver. The first time the child saw this New York City journalist on the evening news in the late 1960s, her jaw dropped.

The woman on the television screen, speaking with such authority, had brown skin like hers. The woman even wore her hair in a sleek, beautiful Afro.

I want to be like her, the child thought. *I want to do what she's doing.*

It wasn't that she wanted to be on television. That didn't even occur to her. But she had grown up reading and watching the news, and now she wanted to write and report the news herself—like Melba Tolliver did.

Even at the tender age of twelve, the girl knew she could do what she set her mind to do. Soon enough, she would head on a path to journalism and never falter. She could have no idea how many places it would take her.

———

Her given name was Gwendolyn Ifill—pronounced like the Eiffel Tower—and she was born in New York City in 1955. Her parents were both from the West Indies. Her mother, Eleanor Husbands Ifill, hailed from Barbados, and her father, O. Urcille Ifill, was from Barbados by way of Panama.

Gwen's father and his brother grew up in poverty and moved to New York together, carried by their strong faith and dreams for the future. They both became ministers and active participants in their new country. Gwen's father was a pastor in the African Methodist Episcopal (AME) Church, and this meant that, about every two years, the family moved to a different parish around the northeast. While this was not

"We can't expect the world to get better by itself. We have to create something we can leave the next generation."

easy for the kids, Gwen learned how to make friends in new places at a young age. Later she would attribute her ease with people she didn't know to these frequent relocations in childhood.

Young Gwen's early years were full of family. The Ifill brothers were close, and so were their children. On Thanksgiving holidays, family get-togethers were crowded, lively, and fun for this preacher's kid. Gwen's family would go back to Queens, New York, where the uncle and his family lived, or her uncle's family would come to wherever Gwen's family lived.

With six children in Gwen's family and ten cousins in her uncle's family, Gwen felt at holidays as if she had fifteen siblings instead of five. Everyone crammed into one house with one bathroom, and all that togetherness simply made them closer. There were hours of playing Scrabble and dominoes, eating good holiday food, and singing together. And there were rousing discussions on politics and justice.

The Ifill elders believed in teaching their children to be informed and to express themselves. They valued education, and attending college was expected for their children. Ultimately, success in life was expected as well. Gwen would have no problem with either. She was always an excellent student, and she graduated from Boston's Simmons College in 1977 with a degree in communications. Then off she went to follow her dream of journalism.

Gwen started her career reporting the news for newspapers. Her first job was an internship with the *Boston Herald-American*. On her first day at work, she found a note on her desk from a fellow staffer— and it wasn't a welcoming note. It called Gwen a racial slur and told her to "go home." But Gwen did not leave. She knew why she was there. She let her supervisor know about the note and went about her work.

Her first jobs were reporting on food. Never mind that she didn't know how to cook—and that's something she laughed about often— there was that curiosity of hers. She knew how to talk to people. She knew that the right questions provided information, and that could affect anything. She had her own formula: "Change comes from listening, learning, caring, and conversation." She went on to report for the *Baltimore Evening Sun*, the *Washington Post*, and the *New York Times*.

Much-loved NBC newscaster Tim Russert persuaded Gwen to consider television reporting. The word had gotten out about her excellence in her field, and she was interviewed by NBC as well as by other networks. In 1994, after much soul-searching, she made the move to television, accepting the offer of the broadcast network she grew up watching. NBC saw brilliance in her journalistic work, and they knew all they had to do was train her how to move from print news to video news. They knew she'd be a quick study. And even though she found the transition challenging, she was successful from the start.

A team worked with Gwen to teach her to slow down her speech for television. She was a fast-talking New Yorker, and she needed to be easier to understand. She also needed to shift her thinking from reporting only words to including visual images. One time, early on, she went on location for a story, wrote it up, and hurried back to the office—only to realize she had completely forgotten to take a cameraperson. But she improved quickly, and once she was on TV, she saw her calls returned more often. Something about being seen on-screen made people agree to talk to her.

After five years with NBC, Gwen found herself with an enticing offer from the Public Broadcasting Service (PBS). This appealed to her, because reporting for a noncommercial network like PBS meant she could do more in-depth reporting. Starting in 1999, she moderated

Washington Week, a show that discussed the news of the week, and she coanchored *Newshour*, first with Jim Lehrer and later with Judy Woodruff. They enjoyed the fact that they were a two-female anchoring team, a rarity in those days, and they became best friends.

Gwen's reporting drew praise from her peers. She was smart and informed. She was civil to her guests. She often felt she was offering a woman's perspective on the news, but she kept her personal views to herself. She knew it was not her job as a journalist to share her opinions, plus she wanted to stay open and curious. She would say her challenge was "to be smarter and more thorough but not to bore people to death."

Gwen's working years were exciting and fulfilling. There were many challenges, but the hardest thing she did, she would say, was to moderate two vice-presidential debates. Her first one was in 2004 between Dick Cheney and John Edwards. It took hard preparation, but it went well.

Her second debate was between Sarah Palin and Joe Biden in 2008. Besides the pressure to perform the evening of the debate, she had just broken her ankle and was in a lot of pain. Since she needed to stay clearheaded and on top of it all, she could not take any medication other than over-the-counter pain relievers. She was helped onstage on crutches. She laid the crutches down and out of sight before the show started. She was hurting, but she muscled through. Fortunately, television viewers never saw the problem.

Gwen would always joke that the best part of moderating those two debates was being portrayed by actress Queen Latifah in *Saturday Night Live* skits. She happened to run into Queen Latifah at an event one evening and told her so!

In 2009, Barack Obama became the first Black president in America. A few years before, Gwen began writing a book on political power and civil rights. The title of the book was *The Breakthrough: Politics and Race in the Age of Obama.* Even though Obama's name was in the subtitle, she had started writing before he was on the presidential horizon. Her publisher, however, decided to release the book on the day of Obama's inauguration. This caused some controversy. Could Gwen, a Black reporter, be trusted to be fair and unbiased in covering the new president when he was a fellow Black American? A reporter asked her as much. Gwen, who believed in never burning bridges, chose not to show offense. She gave the reporter an even-keeled answer: "I'm still capable of looking at his pros and cons in a political sense." She also added, "No one's ever assumed a white reporter can't cover a white candidate."

Gwen was a single, working woman moving at a fast pace. But that didn't dictate her entire life. She had many close friends, and often entertained them at her home with dinner, games of Scrabble, sing-alongs, and lots of fun. Journalist John Dickerson would say, "You could read by the light of her smile. And if you could make her laugh, that was . . . the sound of pure joy." You can find interviews with Gwen online and hear her hearty laughter, something her friends relished.

She was an active member of her church, the Metropolitan African Methodist Episcopal Church of Washington, DC. Of course, she had grown up as a preacher's kid in this denomination. But it was also important to her that this historic downtown church had been a haven so many years ago for runaway slaves.

Gwen often claimed that her proudest moment was the day she was part of a Martin Luther King Jr. celebration in Washington and found herself sharing the stage with every living civil rights leader she'd watched on TV while growing up. What a thrill! How she wished her parents could see this, but by then, they had both passed on. She knew they would have been so pleased.

A particularly rewarding part of Gwen's life in journalism was how many times young Black girls would approach her, telling her that they watched her on TV and wanted to be a journalist too. At those times, Gwen realized the power of having her image on the screen. She knew she was there not only to report and discuss the news openly, honestly, and courteously but to provide a living example and inspiration for these girls.

On November 14, 2016, Gwen Ifill—so full of life and brilliance and fun—died of complications from cancer while surrounded by her loving family and friends. She was sixty-one. Thousands attended her funeral, held at the church she had attended for the past seventeen years. The *New York Times* covered the event, which lasted almost three hours, and published a tribute to Gwen, headlining it "Thousands of Mourners Celebrate Gwen Ifill's Tenacity and Grace."

What a legacy she left. As moderator of *Washington Week*, she had become the first Black woman (and the youngest person) to host a major talk show on politics. She was half of the first female duo to coanchor the nightly news. She had won so many journalism awards that her office wall was covered with them. Gwen was a modern American success story in every way, from being the child of immigrants, to fighting racism and sexism as she achieved her goals, to presenting herself as strong, brilliant, and classy. Gone too soon, yes. But living on in future reporters.

Cousin Sherrilyn Ifill spoke passionately about Gwen, noting that her warm presence on camera somehow made viewers believe they knew her. She described her cousin as "she of the shining eyes and killer cheekbones and megawatt smile." When, in February 2020, a postage stamp was issued with Gwen Ifill's image, it pictured her exactly as her cousin described her.

LET'S REVIEW

1. What person on television was Gwen's first inspiration for her own future?
2. Why were Gwen's reporting skills questioned when President Obama was elected?
3. Gwen attended a Washington, DC, church of the same denomination she was raised in. What other compelling reason did she have for liking this church?

LET'S DO MORE

Gwen hosted two debates between four vice-presidential candidates. What presidential candidates did each run with? Do you think such televised debates are important? Why or why not?

DIG DEEPER
Questions and Activities

- The title of this book is *She Led the Way*. How did each woman profiled lead her way, and how do we benefit today?

- Make a time line from Ellen Craft's birth on through Gwen Ifill's death. On the time line, show the dates of birth and death of all fourteen women in this book. Now add in other historical details, such as American wars, important laws, the end of slavery, and so forth. Fill in some details from these women's lives in the appropriate years. Feel free to illustrate where you wish. When you look at your time line, can you draw any conclusions about the lives of Blacks in America? What can you learn?

- When were Southern slaves freed by the Emancipation Proclamation? Who in the book gained her freedom differently? How so?

- What was the Great Migration? When did it take place? How many of the women in this book took part in it?

- We know for certain that two of the women in this book knew each other. Who were they? Do you think some of the other women would have met? Who are they? Why and under what circumstances might they have met?

- Would you like to know any of these women and have a conversation with her? Who and why? What would you ask her?

SOURCES

Note: in alphabetical order by subject's last name.

Atwater

"The Best of Enemies—Now Playing." YouTube video, 0:30. Uploaded by Entract Films, April 16, 2019. https://www.youtube.com/watch?v=oN5NWfhVsNA.

Davidson, Osha Gray. *The Best of Enemies: Race and Redemption in the New South*, movie edition. Chapel Hill: University of North Carolina Press, 2019.

Davis, Kelcie. "Ann G. Atwater (1935–2016)." Black Past. November 22, 2018. https://www.blackpast.org/african-american-history/atwater-ann-g-1935-2016/.

History vs. Hollywood. "The Best of Enemies (2019)." History vs. Hollywood, accessed October 7, 2021. https://www.historyvshollywood.com/reelfaces/best-of-enemies/.

"Meet the Real Ann Atwater from 'The Best of Enemies.'" YouTube video, 5:28. Uploaded by School for Conversion, January 19, 2019. https://www.youtube.com/watch?v=emR_N7yLVbU.

NC Department of Natural and Cultural Resources. "Activist Ann Atwater." NC Department of Natural and Cultural Resources, accessed October 7, 2021. https://www.ncdcr.gov/blog/2020/01/28/activist-ann-atwater.

"Taraji P. Henson and Sam Rockwell on the True Story behind 'The Best of Enemies' / GMA." YouTube video, 7:21. Uploaded by *Good Morning America*, April 4, 2019. https://www.youtube.com/watch?v=RIUZ1YI8zkY.

Wikipedia. "Ann Atwater." Wikipedia, accessed October 7, 2021. https://en.wikipedia.org/wiki/Ann_Atwater.

Wikipedia. "C. P. Ellis." Wikipedia, accessed October 7, 2021. https://en.wikipedia.org/wiki/C._P._Ellis.

Bridges

Bridges, Ruby. *This Is Your Time*. New York: Delacorte Press, 2020.

Conroy, Michael. "Ruby Bridges Meets with Marshal Who Escorted Her." *The Herald Bulletin*, September 6, 2013. https://www.heraldbulletin.com /archives/ruby-bridges-meets-with-marshal-who-escorted-her/article _66840a30-b856-5aa3-9c6b-253182e52439.html.

Crowther, Linnea. "Lucille Bridges (1934–2020), Mother in 1960 School Desegregation." Legacy, November 12, 2020. https://www.legacy.com/news/celeb rity-deaths/lucille-bridges-1934-2020-mother-in-1960-school-desegregation/.

Disney. "Ruby Bridges." Disney+, accessed October 7, 2021. https://www.disneyplus.com/movies/ruby-bridges/jMLj7URq8aDA.

Disney. "Ruby Bridges Clip." Disney+, accessed October 7, 2021. https:// www.disneyplus.com/video/ec30702d-dc2a-4182-bf90-00ef9ddafd08.

DuckDuckGo. "Images for Ruby Bridges Painting." Searchresults, October 7, 2021, https://duckduckgo.com/?q=Ruby+Bridges+painting&atb=v223-1&ia =web.

Neuman, Scott. "Lucille Bridges, Mother of Anti-Segregation Icon Ruby Bridges, Dies at 86." NPR, November 11, 2020. https://www.npr.org/2020 /11/11/933854762/lucille-bridges-mother-of-anti-segregation-icon-ruby -bridges-dies-at-86.

"Robert Coles Speaks on Ruby Bridges." YouTube video, 5:23. Uploaded by Colette Ouattara, May 5, 2013. https://www.youtube.com/watch ?v=XPK3zQM2dHU.

"Ruby Bridges: A Marshal's Perspective." YouTube video, 13:01. Uploaded by The Children's Museum of Indianapolis, January 7, 2015. https://www .youtube.com/watch?v=hsCWpXx6ToY.

"Ruby's Journey to School." *Ruby Nell Bridges: The Journey*, accessed October 7, 2021. https://sites.google.com/site/rubynellbridgesthejourney/ruby -s-journey-to-school.

Wikipedia. "Ruby Bridges." Wikipedia, accessed October 7, 2021. https://en .wikipedia.org/wiki/Ruby_Bridges.

Burke

Brandman, Mariana. "Selma Burke (1900–1995)." National Women's History Museum, accessed October 7, 2021. https://www.womenshistory.org /education-resources/biographies/selma-burke.

Epiphany's Spectrums of Ebony. "Dr. Selma Burke." *Our Unsung Story*, March 10, 2017. https://ourunsungstory.blogspot.com/2017/03/dr-selma-burke.html.

Felicien, Bria. "Selma Burke: Sculptor's Influence Seen in FDR's Image on U.S. Dime." *Atlanta Journal-Constitution*, February 6, 2020. https://www.ajc.com/entertainment/arts--theater/selma-burke-sculptor-influence-seen-fdr-image-dime/OBvKKJqGeytPE1hyVmNoZJ/.

Mack, Felicia. "Selma Hortense Burke (1900–1995)." Black Past, December 15, 2007. https://www.blackpast.org/african-american-history/burke-selma-hortense-1900-1995/.

NC Department of Natural and Cultural Resources. "Selma Burke, Renowned for FDR Portrait on the Dime." NC Department of Natural and Cultural Resources, accessed October 7, 2021. https://www.ncdcr.gov/blog/2015/12/31/selma-burke-renowned-fdr-portrait-on-the-dime.

Phelps, Shirelle. "Selma Burke: Reexamining the Dime." *Gale International*, February 17, 2021. https://blog.gale.com/selma-burke-reexamining-the-dime/.

Wikipedia. "Selma Burke." Wikipedia, accessed October 7, 2021. https://en.wikipedia.org/wiki/Selma_Burke.

Coachman

Berry, Daina Ramey, and Kali Nicole Gross. *A Black Women's History of the United States*. Boston: Beacon Press, 2020.

Olympics.com. "Alice Coachman, The First Woman of Colour to Win Athletics Gold." *Olympics Athletics News*, accessed October 7, 2021. https://www.olympic.org/news/alice-coachman-athletics.

Walker, Rhiannon. "The Day Alice Coachman Became the First Black Woman to Win Olympic Gold." *The Undefeated*, August 8, 2018. https://theundefeated.com/features/alice-coachman-became-the-first-black-woman-to-win-olympic-gold-1948-games-in-london/.

Wikipedia. "Alice Coachman." Wikipedia, accessed October 7, 2021. https://en.wikipedia.org/wiki/Alice_Coachman.

Coleman

"Actress Madeline McCray on Bessie Coleman and 'A Dream to Fly: Inspired by the Life Bessie Coleman.'" YouTube video, 15:15. Uploaded by

Madeline McCray, January 8, 2014. https://www.youtube.com/watch ?v=Kb1REHTO26U.

"Bessie Coleman 'A Dream to Fly' by Leslie Harris." YouTube video, 8:21. Uploaded by Jerard Washington, March 5, 2021. https://www.youtube .com/watch?v=ekyejdBVWXk.

"Bessie Coleman—An American Hero." YouTube video, 13:34. Uploaded by TheAvWriter, May 2, 2012. https://www.youtube.com/watch?v=jYYy -dT4498.

The Black Heritage Commemorative Society. "The Complete Collection of Black American Stamps." Black History Stamps, accessed October 8, 2021. www.blackhistorystamps.com.

Tallman, Jill. "Bessie Coleman's Journey to Flight." AOPA, June 12, 2013. https://blog.aopa.org/aopa/tag/bessie-coleman/.

Unladylike2020. "Bessie Coleman: First African American Woman Aviator." Unladylike Productions, accessed October 8, 2021. https://unladylike2020 .com/profile/bessie-coleman/.

Collins

Britannica Kids. "Marva Collins." Britannica Kids, accessed October 7, 2021. https://kids.britannica.com/students/article/Marva-Collins/310771.

Collins, Marva, and Civia Tamarkin. *Marva Collins' Way: Returning to Excellence in Education*. New York: Penguin-Putman, 1982.

Encyclopedia of World Biography. "Marva Collins Biography." *Encyclopedia of World Biography*, accessed October 7, 2021. https://www.notable biographies.com/Co-Da/Collins-Marva.html.

It's All Pink. "Marva Collins: On a Mission." *Pink*, accessed October 8, 2021. https://itsallpink.com/featured-women/item/marva-collins.

"Success! The Marva Collins Approach." YouTube video, 28:07. Uploaded by reelblack, June 18, 2014. https://www.youtube.com /watch?v=yXIDVjDlXpc.

Thompson, Erica. "'This Kind of Beauty . . .'—Prince's 'Most Beautiful' Women." *A Purple Day in December*, May 20, 2019. http://www .apurpledayindecember.com/2019/05/this-kind-of-beauty-princes-most .html.

Wikipedia. "Marva Collins." Wikipedia, accessed October 7, 2021. https://en .wikipedia.org/wiki/Marva_Collins.

Craft

Craft, William. *Running a Thousand Miles for Freedom; or, the Escape of William and Ellen Craft from Slavery*. London: William Tweedie, 1860.

Holmes, Marian Smith. "The Great Escape from Slavery of Ellen and William Craft." *Smithsonian*, June 16, 2010. https://www.smithsonianmag.com/history/the-great-escape-from-slavery-of-ellen-and-william-craft-497960/.

"How William and Ellen Craft Escaped Slavery: Georgia Stories." YouTube video, 7:58. Uploaded by GPB Education, March 16, 2020. https://www.youtube.com/watch?v=n7IYSdo6fMk.

McCaskill, Barbara. *Love, Liberation, and Escaping Slavery: William and Ellen Craft in Cultural Memory*. The University of Georgia Press, 2015.

"William and Ellen Craft: The Slaves that Acted Their Way to Freedom! Hiding in Plain Sight!" YouTube video, 11:51. Uploaded by Chris Fahmy, February 17, 2020. https://www.youtube.com/watch?v=7W5fewb0GZ4.

Young, Jeffrey Robert. "Slavery in Antebellum Georgia." *New Georgia Encyclopedia*, last modified September 30, 2020. https://www.georgiaencyclopedia.org/articles/history-archaeology/slavery-antebellum-georgia.

Crumpler

Carlton, Genevieve. "The Story of Rebecca Lee Crumpler, the First Black Woman to Become a Doctor in American History." All That's Interesting, last modified July 26, 2021. https://allthatsinteresting.com/rebecca-lee-crumpler.

Crumpler, Rebecca Lee. "A Book of Medical Discourses: In Two Parts." *Internet Archive*, accessed October 8, 2021. https://archive.org/details/67521160R.nlm.nih.gov.

Ferry, Georgina. "Rebecca Lee Crumpler: First Black Woman Physician in the USA." *Lancet*, February 13, 2021. https://www.thelancet.com/journals/lancet/article/PIIS0140-6736(21)00301-9/fulltext.

Herbison, Matt. "Is That Dr. Rebecca Lee Crumpler? Misidentification, Copyright, and Pesky Historical Details." *The Legacy Center*, June 2013. https://drexel.edu/legacy-center/blog/overview/2013/june/is-that-dr-rebecca-lee-crumpler-misidentification-copyright-and-pesky-historical-details/.

National Library of Medicine. "Dr. Rebecca Lee Crumpler." *Changing the Face of Medicine*, accessed October 11, 2021. https://cfmedicine.nlm.nih.gov/physicians/biography_73.html.

Resilient Sisterhood Project. "Acknowledging Dr. Rebecca Crumpler." *Resilient Sisterhood Project*, June 22, 2021. https://www.rsphealth.org/dr-rebecca -crumpler.

Shelf Awareness. "Reading with . . . Perri Klass." *Shelf Awareness*, March 17, 2021. https://www.shelf-awareness.com/issue.html?issue=3944#m51761, https://www.nps.gov/people/dr-rebecca-lee-crumpler.htm.

Wikipedia. "Rebecca Lee Crumpler." *Wikipedia*, accessed October 7, 2021. https://en.wikipedia.org/wiki/Rebecca_Lee_Crumpler.

Ifill

Alcindor, Yamiche. "Thousands of Mourners Celebrate Gwen Ifill's Tenacity and Grace." *New York Times*, November 20, 2016. https://www.nytimes .com/2016/11/20/us/gwen-ifill-funeral.html.

Biography. "Gwen Ifill Biography (1955–)." *Biography*, accessed October 7, 2021. https://web.archive.org/web/20081001051535/http://www.biogra phy.com/search/article.do?id=212144.

Elassar, Alaa. "Postal Service Honors Pioneering Journalist Gwen Ifill with a Black Heritage Forever Stamp." CNN, February 1, 2020. https://www.cnn .com/2020/02/01/us/gwen-ifill-stamp-black-heritage-month-trnd/index.html.

"Gwen Ifill on Being a Little Girl Transfixed by News." YouTube video, 6:27. Uploaded by PBS NewsHour, November 14, 2016. https://www.youtube .com/watch?v=5iUG9S72GvU.

Ifill, Sherrilyn. "Remembering Gwen Ifill: Truth Teller and Exemplar of Ci- vility." *American Prospect*, December 3, 2016. https://prospect.org/culture /remembering-gwen-ifill-truth-teller-exemplar-civility/.

Simmons University. "Meet Gwen Ifill." Simmons University, accessed October 8, 2021. https://www.simmons.edu/academics/colleges-schools -departments/ifill/meet-gwen-ifill.

Sutton, Kelsey, and Hadas Gold. "Gwen Ifill Dead at Age 61." *Politico*, No- vember 14, 2016. https://www.politico.com/blogs/on-media/2016/11/gwen -ifill-dies-at-age-61-231347.

Television Academy Foundation. "Gwen Ifill: Journalist." *The Interviews*, ac- cessed October 8, 2021. https://interviews.televisionacademy.com/inter views/gwen-ifill.

Wikipedia. "Melba Toliver." *Wikipedia*, accessed October 7, 2021. https://en .wikipedia.org/wiki/Melba_Tolliver.

Johnson

Davis, Jonnelle. "Daughter of NASA Mathematician Portrayed in 'Hidden Figures' Talks about 'Smart but Humble' Mom." *News & Record*, January 16, 2017. https://greensboro.com/news/local_news/daughter-of-nasa-mathematician-portrayed-in-hidden-figures-talks-about-smart-but-humble-mom/article_a14b217f-e216-54a7-99fa-f3dc41901c2b.html.

Editors of Encyclopaedia Britannica. "Katherine Johnson: American Mathematician." *Britannica*, accessed October 8, 2021. https://www.britannica.com/biography/Katherine-Johnson-mathematician.

Hodges, Jim. "She Was a Computer When Computers Wore Skirts." NASA, August 26, 2008. https://www.nasa.gov/centers/langley/news/researchernews/rn_kjohnson.html.

Johnson, Katherine, with Joylette Hylick and Katherine Moore. *My Remarkable Journey: A Memoir*. New York: HarperCollins, 2021.

"Katherine Johnson Biography." The Famous People, accessed October 8, 2021. https://www.thefamouspeople.com/profiles/katherine-johnson-22835.php.

Kids Encyclopedia Facts. "Katherine Johnson Facts for Kids." *Kiddle Encyclopedia*, accessed October 8, 2021. https://kids.kiddle.co/Katherine_Johnson.

Krishna, Swapna, and Kelsey McConnell. "10 Extraordinary Facts about Katherine Johnson, the Late Groundbreaking 'Human Computer.'" *The Portalist*, February 8, 2019. https://theportalist.com/5-extraordinary-facts-about-katherine-johnson.

Labrie, Sarah. "Hidden Figures Character: Katherine Coleman Goble Johnson." *LitCharts*, January 9, 2018. https://www.litcharts.com/lit/hidden-figures/characters/katherine-coleman-goble-johnson.

Shetterly, Margot Lee. *Hidden Figures: The American Dream and the Untold Story of the Black Women Who Helped Win the Space Race*. New York: William Morrow & Company, 2016.

Shetterly, Margot Lee, with Winifred Conkling. *Hidden Figures: The True Story of Four Black Women and the Space Race*. Illustrated by Laura Freeman. New York: HarperCollins, 2018.

Smither, William. "Katherine Goble Johnson (1918–2020)." Black Past, January 6, 2017. https://www.blackpast.org/african-american-history/johnson-katherine-g-1918/.

Vitug, Eric, ed. "Katherine G. Johnson." NASA, May 25, 2017. https://www
.nasa.gov/feature/katherine-g-johnson.

Wikipedia. "Katherine Johnson." Wikipedia, accessed October 7, 2021.
https://en.wikipedia.org/wiki/Katherine_Johnson.

Younghans, Samantha Faragalli. "Katherine Johnson Wasn't Just a
Mathematician—She Was Also a Mom to Three Daughters." Distractify,
February 24, 2020. https://www.distractify.com/p/katherine-johnson-kids.

Taylor

Dell, Pamela. *Memoir of Susie King Taylor: A Civil War Nurse.* North
Mankato, MN: Capstone Press, 2017.

Margaritoff, Marco. "Meet Susie King Taylor, the First African American Army
Nurse Who Moonlit as a Teacher for Black Union Soldiers." All That's Interesting, October 15, 2020. https://allthatsinteresting.com/susie-king-taylor.

National Library of Medicine. "Susie King Taylor: Teacher, Nurse, Author."
Binding Wounds, Pushing Boundaries (exhibit), accessed October 8, 2021.
https://www.nlm.nih.gov/exhibition/bindingwounds/pdfs/BioKingTaylor
OB130.pdf.

Taylor, Susie King. "Reminiscences of My Life in Camp with the 33d United
States Colored Troops Late 1st S. C. Volunteers," electronic edition. *Docu-
menting the American South*, accessed October 7, 2021. https://docsouth
.unc.edu/neh/taylorsu/taylorsu.html.

U.S. National Park Service. "Susie King Taylor." U.S. National Park Service, accessed October 8, 2021. https://www.nps.gov/people/susie-king-taylor.htm.

Wikipedia. "Susie Taylor." Wikipedia, accessed October 7, 2021. https://en
.wikipedia.org/wiki/Susie_Taylor.

Tyson

CBC Radio. "How Cicely Tyson Paved the Way for Complex and Layered
Black Storytelling in Hollywood." CBC, January 26, 2021. https://www
.cbc.ca/radio/q/tuesday-jan-26-2021-cicely-tyson-larnell-lewis-and-more
-1.5886953/how-cicely-tyson-paved-the-way-for-complex-and-layered
-black-storytelling-in-hollywood-1.5886969.

"Cicely Tyson's Medal of Freedom from Obama in 2016." YouTube video,
0:47. Uploaded by NowThis News, January 29, 2021. https://www.youtube
.com/watch?v=ga1xmHHwRYs.

Klemesrud, Judy. "Cicely, the Looker." *New York Times*, October 1, 1972. https://www.nytimes.com/1972/10/01/archives/cicely-the-looker-from -sounder-cicely-the-looker.html.

McFadden, Robert D. "Cicely Tyson, an Actress Who Shattered Stereo-types, Dies at 96." *New York Times*, January 28, 2021. https://www.ny times.com/2021/01/28/obituaries/cicely-tyson-dead.html.

Tyson, Cicely, with Michelle Burford. *Just As I Am*. New York: HarperCollins, 2021.

Wikipedia. "Cicely Tyson." Wikipedia, accessed October 7, 2021. https://en .wikipedia.org/wiki/Cicely_Tyson.

Waddles

"Black Women Oral History Project. Interviews, 1976–1981. Charleszetta Waddles. OH-31. Schlesinger Library." Cambridge: Radcliffe Institute, Harvard University. Harvard Library Viewer, accessed October 11, 2021. https://iiif.lib.harvard.edu/manifests/view/drs:45177052$8i.

Boyd, Herb. "The Rev. Charleszetta 'Mother' Waddles, Fed the Body and the Soul." *New York Amsterdam News*, August 24, 2017. http://m.amsterdam news.com/news/2017/aug/24/rev-charleszetta-mother-waddles-fed-body -and-soul/.

Brief Biographies. "Charleszetta 'Mother' Waddles Biography." *Brief Biogra-phies*, accessed October 11, 2021. https://biography.jrank.org/pages/2490 /Waddles-Charleszetta-Mother.html.

"Mother Waddles 'God Needs People to Stand in for Him.' Loaves of Bread Story That Multiplied." YouTube video, 1:02. Uploaded by AMO Produc-tions, April 22, 2017. https://www.youtube.com/watch?v=JKlDJsmT6Ts.

Saed, Omnia. "The Poetry-Loving Cook Who Fed Detroit's Soul." *Atlas Obscura*, June 17, 2021. https://www.atlasobscura.com/articles/mother -waddles-detroit.

Wikipedia. "Charleszetta Waddles." Wikipedia, accessed October 7, 2021. https://en.wikipedia.org/wiki/Charleszetta_Waddles.

Walker

BBC. "Madam CJ Walker: 'An Inspiration to Us All.'" BBC, April 5, 2020. https://www.bbc.com/news/business-52130592.

BlackThen. "You Can't Take Our Crowns: The Impact of Slavery on Black Women's Hair." *BlackThen*, September 8, 2019. https://blackthen.com/you-cant-take-our-crowns-the-impact-of-slavery-on-black-womens-hair/.

Bundles, A'Lelia. *On Her Ground: The Life and Times of Madam C. J. Walker.* New York: Simon & Schuster, 2001.

Encyclopedia of World Biography. "Madame C. J. Walker Biography." *Encyclopedia of World Biography*, accessed October 11, 2021. https://www.notablebiographies.com/Tu-We/Walker-Madame-C-J.html.

Gates, Henry Louis Jr. "Madam Walker, the First Black American Woman to Be a Self-Made Millionaire." PBS, accessed October 11, 2021. https://www.pbs.org/wnet/african-americans-many-rivers-to-cross/history/100-amazing-facts/madam-walker-the-first-black-american-woman-to-be-a-self-made-millionaire/.

Jenkins, Beverly. "Get to Know Madam C. J. Walker, America's 1st Female Millionaire!" Inspire More, February 16, 2021. https://www.inspiremore.com/madam-cj-walker/.

Joachim, Rébecca. "Natural Hair: The History before the Movement." *Kika Curls*, August 2, 2017. https://www.kikacurls.com/blogs/kikas-blog/natural-hair-the-history-before-the-movement.

McLeod, Nia Simone. "Madam C. J. Walker Quotes Celebrating the Self-Made Millionaire." Everyday Power, November 13, 2020. https://everydaypower.com/madam-c-j-walker-quotes/.

Thirteen.org. "Slave Women and the Head-Wrap." *The Slave Experience: Men, Women, and Gender*, accessed October 11, 2021. https://www.thirteen.org/wnet/slavery/experience/gender/feature6.html.

"The True Story of Madam C. J. Walker: Two Dollars and a Dream." YouTube video, 51:12. Uploaded by WORLD Channel, March 31, 2020. https://www.youtube.com/watch?v=WrpVozNIHds.

Uhai Haircare. "Hair & History: A Short Story on the Evolution of Hair in the African American Community." *At the Root*, February 4, 2020. https://uhaihair.com/blogs/news/hair-history-a-short-story-on-the-evolution-of-hair-in-the-african-american-community.

Wikipedia. "Madam C. J. Walker." Wikipedia, accessed October 7, 2021. https://en.wikipedia.org/wiki/Madam_C._J._Walker.

SUZANNE CURTIS BRIGGS is a former teacher who has been reading history all her life and enjoys writing about it. She loves a good story, especially when it's true.